PREACHING IS BELIEVING
THE SERMON
AS THEOLOGICAL REFLECTION

Ronald J. Allen

Westminster John Knox Press
LOUISVILLE • LONDON

Book design by Sharon Adams
Cover design by Lisa Buckley

First edition
Published by Westminster John Knox Press
Louisville, Kentucky

This book is printed on acid-free paper that meets the American National Standards Institute Z39.48 standard. ∞

PRINTED IN THE UNITED STATES OF AMERICA

02 03 04 05 06 07 08 09 10 11 – 10 9 8 7 6 5 4 3 2 1

Library of Congress Cataloging-in-Publication Data

Allen, Ronald J. (Ronald James), date
    Preaching is believing : the sermon as theological,
    reflection / Ronald J. Allen.
        p. cm.
    Includes bibliographical references and index.
    ISBN 0-664-22330-3 (alk. paper)
    1. Doctrinal preaching.   I. Title.

    BV4235.D63 A55 2001
    251—dc21   2001056768

For
Clark M. Williamson
Whose Life Embodies the Way of Blessing of the God of Israel

Contents

Introduction

After worship one Sunday, I was in the parlor of our local congregation munching stale doughnut holes while talking with another member. My companion grew up in a religiously conservative congregation in which the preaching mediated a distinct and systematic theological point of view from week to week.

My friend reflected, "While there were problems with the theology of that preacher and congregation, I came away with a coherent picture of what it means to be a Christian. Things fit together. I knew what was important and why. As my open spirit and education moved me toward congregations that are more liberal, I miss that systematic quality in the preaching. If you asked me, on the basis of the preaching, to give a systematic statement of what our church believes, I'm not sure I could. Sometimes we get a theology of the week—today Matthew, next week Mark, and John the week after that." We recalled persons in our congregation puzzling over how to make theological sense of difficult experiences, and over troubling passages from the Bible. At the bell to begin Bible school, my friend concluded, "We need preaching that is more than a theology of the week. We need preaching that will help us catch a vision of how God relates with every atom in the universe and how we can live in response."

Preaching Is Believing calls for sermons to help congregations move toward such theological clarity. In this book I join David

1

Buttrick and Edward Farley, who taught at Vanderbilt University, in hoping that preaching today will "take a turn toward theology."[1] In particular, I urge preachers to give systematic theology a higher profile in preaching because systematic theology helps the congregation name what we believe and make coherent sense of life from the perspective of God so that the community can live and witness with integrity. As the title of the book suggests, preaching is itself an act of believing. The sermon bodies forth the deepest beliefs of the congregation . . . *and the preacher* . . . in a context of theological reflection.

I explore two ways preachers can move in this direction: (1) by increasing the visibility of systematic theology in sermons that originate with a biblical text, and (2) by preaching sermons that start and move as systematic theology. This book is not a major theoretical work, but is rather a practical handbook to enable the preacher to help the congregation grasp the core of Christian conviction as well as the roots and implications of such conviction. I hope that such preaching will help the congregation catch a vision of how God relates in love and justice with each and every atom of the universe.

This book walks a delicate line. It invites all preachers, regardless of theological orientation, to bring systematic theology to greater explicit prominence in the pulpit. The volume does not promote a particular approach to systematic theology. This exploration focuses more on the formal work of systematic theology in relationship to preaching than on the material content of theology. However, the latter is not far away. Each systematic theology contains its own theological claims and methods. From one volume of systematic theology to another, these claims and methods differ.

Some readers may object that my approach to theology is hopelessly conventional, especially given the innovations in theological method and content that have emerged from the various liberation and contextual theologies, and the postmodern dual emphases of resistance to systematization and celebration of pluralism. I reply that while the genre and methods of systematic theology may not be sacred, they have a proven record of helping some sectors of the church clarify what they believe and how to live in response. That this approach has had some unfortunate chapters in its history does not completely obviate it. The postmodern pluralism of theologies has a place for continuing the tradition of systematic theology, though in dialogue with other methods. In any event, I do not regard my approach as imperial. A good systematic theology is open to fresh insights into Christian belief, theological method, and relationship to its context, as well as principles for its own correction. I believe that persons can take up the general call of this book—for preachers to make our theological convictions and methods more explicit in preaching—from a variety of theological methods and points of view.

My own theology moves in the revisionary theological stream (emphasizing conversation and mutual critical correlation) with an orientation toward process (relational) theology. These motifs inevitably inform the present work, but this book is not designed as a primer for preaching revisionary theology. I take a formal approach to encourage preachers from the spectrum of theological families (outlined in the Appendix) to bring their perspectives more boldly to the surface of the sermon. Even when I do not consider particular theological systems or claims to be adequate, I try to treat them with respect. My goal is that the book will be accessible to preachers in the broad world of contemporary theologies while recognizing that aspects of the book will be uncomfortable to some readers.

Furthermore, preacherly circles today often describe theology as second-order language in contrast to first-order language. In this way of thinking, first-order communication is said to be personal, experiential, and often in the form of story, while second-order language is said to be abstract, conceptual, reflective, often in the form of propositions, and one step removed from experience. While this division has some heuristic value in helping us see that systematic theology provides categories that interpret experience, it obscures the fact that the concepts, explanation, and propositions of systematic theology can generate primary experience. Furthermore, I must candidly say that what passes for first-order language in sermons is sometimes emotionally evocative but intellectually empty.

What a community believes about God and other theological matters is deeply existential and has significant ethical consequences. I am deeply moved by preaching that brings theological concepts to life in ways described in chapter 5. Preachers who become more overtly theological should see themselves not as abandoning so-called first-order language for second-order, but rather as tapping into the full gamut of human awareness. Primary experience is interpreted by critical reflection that in turn becomes a part of, and deepens, primary experience.

In this book I do not directly take up the important matter of developing a theology *of* preaching. I focus specifically on preaching theological content. Chapter 1 asks, "What is systematic theology?" Chapter 2 sketches five reasons for giving significant attention to systematic theology in the pulpit today. Chapter 3 considers the roles of systematic theology when the preacher develops a sermon based on a text from the Bible. Chapter 4 moves in the tradition of topical preaching by suggesting that the preacher can sometimes develop sermons that are expositions of particular theological convictions without basing the sermon on a particular biblical text. A conviction from systematic theology can serve as the foundation of the sermon in a way similar to a biblical text serving as the foundation of an expository sermon. Chapter 5 posits strategies for making systematic theology interesting in the sermon. Chapter 6 invites ministers to integrate systematic theology into whatever calendar of preaching they follow (Christian year and selected lectionary, *lectio continua*, or free selection of texts). The final chapter offers two sample sermons that illustrate preaching with a conscientious and heightened attention to systematic theological concerns. One sermon, on the ascension of Jesus in Acts 1:6–11, is expository (thus illustrating motifs from chapter 3) while the other is on baptism (thus relating to chapter 4). The Appendix charts the relationship of historic and contemporary theological families. In the Bibliography I list selected contemporary discussions that relate preaching and systematic theology.

I hope the effects of this book avoid "the law of unintended consequences." According to this wise principle, which I learned from Clark M. Williamson, dean of Christian Theological

Seminary, every thought and initiative has consequences that its initiator(s) did not intend. In particular, I hope that my clarion for more clear and cogent statements of systematic theology in the pulpit does not feed the fire of a wooden, uncritical authoritarianism.

I thank the Writer's Group at Christian Theological Seminary for reflecting critically on the working outline from which I wrote. This interdisciplinary group, consisting of Charles Allen (systematic theology), Brian Grant (pastoral counseling), Holly Hearon (Second Testament), Felicity Kelcourse (pastoral counseling), Dan Moseley (Christian ministries), Marti Steussy (First Testament), Newell Williams (church history), and Clark Williamson (systematic theology), models the kind of theological acuity that this book seeks in preaching and in all areas of ecclesial life. Where I have not followed their advice, I am at theological risk.

1

Systematic Theology
as a Pastoral Resource

When I told a friend in pastoral ministry that I was about to write a book on preaching systematic theology, that person replied, "That sounds dull." At one level, I find it hard to imagine how anyone could find systematic theology dull. Theology, after all, deals with the most existentially important questions in life, questions such as: Who am I, why am I here, and what am I to do? How can people live together in mutuality, respect, and with abundance for all? Why can we believe that God exists? What can a Christian say in the face of innocent suffering? What can we affirm about life after death?

Nonetheless, at another level, I understand my friend's attitude. Books and lectures in systematic theology do not always help readers catch the living connection between theology and the everyday world. Occasional volumes of systematic theology are hard to understand. I once knew a systematic theologian who seemed to regard obfuscation as a vocation.

In this chapter I affirm that systematic theology has direct pastoral value for the preacher. I begin with the basic question, "What is systematic theology?" Then I meditate on the relationship between systematic theologians and systematic theology, and pause to consider the relationship between systematic theology and doctrine. After a presentation on theological criteria in the everyday life of the congregation, I consider the preacher's theological task in relationship to intuitive theology.

WHAT IS SYSTEMATIC THEOLOGY?

The term "systematic theology" refers broadly to the attempt to make a logical, coherent, comprehensive interpretation of what a Christian community believes (or can believe) about essential elements of Christian faith and life.[1] Systematic theology not only helps the Christian community clarify its beliefs, but also helps the community discern how to act in the world, for theology empowers mission.[2] Ellen Charry, a noted contemporary theologian, notices that theology helps people develop into the kind of persons and communities that God wants us to be.[3]

Systematic theology tends to give a sequential summary of basic beliefs according to category, for example, God, Jesus Christ, the Holy Spirit, the church, and the world. Such theology helps the church come to a clear statement of beliefs concerning at least the following: the nature of human perception, the nature and sources of our perception of God, basic beliefs about the nature and activity of God, the nature of the cosmos, the nature of human beings, the nature and purpose of human community as well as the relationship of humankind with nature, the nature and work of Jesus Christ, the Holy Spirit, the Trinity, the nature and purpose of the church, faith, grace, salvation, the practice of Christian life and community (e.g., worship, prayer, baptism, the breaking of the loaf), how Christian faith relates to other religions, the mission of the church in the larger world, eschatology. Systematic theology shows how these elements work together, helps the community identify qualities that are theologically necessary for Christian life, and helps the community reflect on the degree to which it manifests this vision.

Systematic theology takes biblical perspectives into account. Yet, even when affirmations of systematic theology begin with biblical passages, theology's affirmations are typically broader than any single biblical passage, or even the sum of passages.

Preachers sometimes resist the very idea of systematic theology. Occasionally, preachers complain that systematic theology tries to explain too much and does not allow sufficient mystery. In a similar vein, a student recently claimed that systematic theology limits God by "locking God in a box of logic." To be sure, finite human beings can never fully understand the infinite God. We need humility with respect to our understandings of God and other theological matters. However, our inability to understand everything about God should not short-circuit our willingness to press as far as we can, recognizing that our theological interpretations are not absolute (if they were, they would be God) but are open to revision. Frankly, I usually hear God described as a mystery when a preacher comes into contact with a knotty theological problem and wants to escape disciplined theological inquiry (or does not know how to do so) by saying, "We can't understand a particular problem. It is a mystery, so we don't have to think about it anymore." As for "locking God in a box of logic," most systematic theologies assume the integrity of God, by which they mean that God cannot do things that contradict one another. The community could not trust a God who engages in contradiction.

The expression "systematic theology" does not, by itself, denote specific theological content. It refers to the attempt to describe foundational Christian doctrines and to show how they relate with one another in such a way that the various elements of Christian conviction do not contradict one another. When Christians engage in systematic theology, they attempt to portray a theological vision that is logically consistent within itself and with our experience in the world. Each systematic theology has its own particular theological content, that is, each systematic theology presents its own view of perception, God, Jesus Christ, the Holy Spirit. Preachers typically develop sermons from the perspective of the particular systematic theology that they find most adequate to explain the relationship between Christian claims and their experience in the world.

Systematic theology is interpretation through and through. A systematic theologian offers an *interpretation* of the foundational matters of theology. Even when a systematic theologian purports only to be summing up basic Christian doctrine, that summary interprets.

Systematic theologians write because something in the world or the church prompts them to offer a fresh interpretation of aspects of Christian vision, or because they think that a traditional element of Christian vision needs to be reemphasized or reframed. Feminist systematic theologians, for instance, interpret the categories of systematic theology from the standpoint of their experience in a patriarchal culture. The sexism of North America prompts them to seek an interpretation of Christian vision that liberates women from repression and that creates a community of equality for all.

SYSTEMATIC THEOLOGIANS
AND SYSTEMATIC THEOLOGY

We often think narrowly of systematic theology as the work of individual theologians, such as Karl Barth, Donald Bloesch, Leonardo Boff, Rita Nakashima Brock, Rebecca Chopp, John Cobb, James Cone, James Evans, Edward Farley, Gustavo Gutierrez, Ada Maria Isasi-Dias, Elisabeth Johnson, Major Jones, Serene Jones, Catherine Mowry LaCugna, John Mac-Quarrie, James McClendon, Sallie McFague, Alister McGrath, Jose Miranda, Jürgen Moltmann, Christopher Morse, Thomas Oden, Wolfhart Pannenberg, William Placher, Karl Rahner, Rosemary Radford Reuther, J. Deotis Roberts, Letty Russell, Juan Segundo, Jon Sobrino, Dorothee Sölle, C. S. Song, Kendall Soulen, Marjorie Suchocki, Paul Tillich, David Tracy, Paul Van Buren, Delores Williams, and Clark Williamson.[4]

In wider-angle vision, systematic theology is associated not just with individual theologians but also with schools of thought that gather around the perspectives of theologians or theological movements, for example, Tillichians, Barthians, or McFaguians. Feminist theologians share common perspectives on perception, God, the world, Christ, the Spirit, and community. Though the feminist community shares many convictions, individual feminists often put forth distinctive points of view. Widening the lens to take account of the full theological spectrum, we note in the Appendix that we can speak of at least eleven historic theological families (e.g., Orthodox, Lutheran, Reformed) that interact with four contemporary theological families (evangelical, postliberal, liberation, revisionary).

As contemporary systematic theology seeks to help the church understand the world from transcendent perspective, it engages in conversation with the Bible and Christian tradition. Christian tradition, of course, is not a monolith but is made up of many theological movements, including Roman Catholicism, Wesleyanism, the Anabaptists, and the Pentecostals. Such movements generate distinctive theological viewpoints. Contemporary systematic theologies often self-consciously seek to interpret their traditions for the sake of the present. Today's Reformed theologian, for instance, engages in the dual interpretation of (1) the present situation from the standpoint of that theology, and (2) Reformed theology from the standpoint of the present situation.

Sometimes churches (and theologians) cast their beliefs in formal statements that are structured systematically. The Westminster Shorter Catechism and John Calvin's *Institutes of the Christian Religion* are examples of such statements. Often, however, a cluster of beliefs grows up over time, and a community accepts them as semi-normative even though the affirmations are not consolidated in an official theological statement.

Theologians often draw positively on these resources, but sometimes criticize them. When traditions or theological statements from the past are inconsistent or inadequate, systematic theology reflects critically to help sort out those elements that are normative and those which are not.

Preachers sometimes link themselves with particular theological movements. For instance, I know preachers who describe themselves as Wesleyans or liberation theologians or postliberals, or Whiteheadians. These pastors interpret God and the world through the lens of the theological movement whose interpretations of Christian vision they find most compelling. However, few pastors, congregations, or systematic theologians are singular in theologian orientation. Even preachers who conscientiously subscribe to a particular theological system typically graft elements from other theologies into their systems. We are nearly all of mixed theological blood.

Once in a while I hear a preacher say something like, "I am not a Whiteheadian or a liberation theologian or a Wesleyan but a Christian." People make such comments to signal that their primary loyalty is not to a theological system but to God. These preachers stand against theological sectarianism. However, human beings are, by nature, interpretive animals. Every act of awareness contains interpretive elements. We do not have access to the gospel in a pure and objective form. Every statement we make about God, Jesus Christ, the Holy Spirit, the church, or the world is an interpretation. Since we cannot achieve an undiluted perception of doctrine, we need to be cognizant and critical of our interpretive lenses whether they are ground on the wheel of a particular systematic theologian, or a theological movement, or some other orienting perspective.

The preacher who claims not to have an interpretive lens through which to understand the Bible and Christian tradition needs to recognize that such a statement *is* an interpretation. Such preachers need to search themselves and their worlds more carefully to determine their actual interpretive assumptions and to reflect critically on them.

The Reformed movement birthed a rubric that should guide all Christian movements when it said that the church is "reformed and always reforming." That is, the church is always in the process of assessing the adequacy of its theological vision. Indeed, a key part of systematic theology is helping the church continuously evaluate its understanding of its tradition, claims, life, and witness.

SYSTEMATIC THEOLOGY AND DOCTRINE

Although systematic theology is intimately related to Christian doctrine, they are different in three ways. First, the term *systematic theology* came into use in the Enlightenment church, whereas the designation "doctrine" is old as the Bible. English versions sometimes translate the Greek word *didaskalia* as doctrine (e.g., Eph. 4:14; 1 Tim. 1:3). *Didaskalia* is from a Greek root that means "teaching." Continuing this emphasis, the English word *doctrine* is a transliteration of the Latin *doctrina*, which also means "teaching." At heart, doctrine is the teaching of what the church believes. The systematic theologian explains and interprets doctrine for particular times and contexts.

Second, the church does not always show how doctrines relate with one another in the way that is central to systematic theology. Doctrines sometimes exist in the church in random relationship. Systematic theology specifically seeks not only to state clearly the core of Christian conviction, but also to order the church's doctrines in a logical fashion, and to make explicit how various parts of doctrine relate with one another.

Third, whereas the church sometimes simply asserts doctrinal beliefs, systematic theology aims to provide a full explanation not only of *what* the church believes, but *why*. Theology reflects specifically on the relationship between doctrine and the historical context of the church. A doctrine is theological shorthand that appears to be sufficient for one historical moment, whereas a later circumstance may prompt the church to reassess, amplify, amend, correct, or reject an aspect of doctrine. Indeed, systematic theology helps the church engage in doctrinal criticism, that is, evaluating "the reliability and adequacy of the doctrinal formulations represented by the Christian tradition,"[5] allowing it to ask, Does a doctrinal affirmation measure up to the best ways the contemporary community, in conversation with tradition, understands God, Christ, Spirit, church, and world?

Doctrine and theology develop over time in response to changing perspectives and circumstances, much like a plant grows.[6] Doctrine begins with the seed of recognition that a particular observation or claim is of fundamental importance to the community of faith. Often, doctrine begins when the church recognizes such an insight in the Bible or in congregational practice. This seed opens and breaks the surface of the soil as the church reflects, sometimes formally but often informally, on the new insight and amplifies it. New historical circumstances or new data function like rainfall that causes the plant to grow by prompting the church to recognize previously unnoticed qualities in the doctrine. Just as the process of photosynthesis enables the plant to live, so fresh observations spawn still more reflection and refinement.

Once in a while, a growing plant will sprout a branch in an odd place. In response to light and space, the branch grows and becomes a disproportionately large part of the plant. Similarly, elements of doctrine sometimes lose immediate contact with the original trunk of discovery and take on a life of their own. Later statements of doctrine can sometimes be as different from the originating impulse as the oak tree is from the acorn. The tree can provide shade and lumber that are impossible for the undeveloped acorn. A windstorm can also rip up the tree and send it crashing into a nearby house. Hence, preacher and congregation need to reflect in a critical and penetrating way on doctrine in its mature form. Later generations, of course, will reflect on the systematic theological formulations of our era and, doubtless, will find some of them adequate, others inadequate, some timely, others quaint.

Systematic theologians help the church interpret the content and implications of the Bible and historic doctrines for the sake of the present. Systematic theology helps the church understand why it is important to reaffirm historic claims. It helps the church respond to questions concerning doctrine and witness. Fresh perspectives that were not available to earlier generations sometimes prompt systematic theologians to reinterpret Christian conviction. Once in a while, systematic theologians conclude that the church needs to correct or reject an element of doctrine.

Doctrine often exists on both a formal and informal level. At the formal level, church bodies often adopt specific doctrine as the official position. At an informal level, some beliefs function as doctrine though they are not formally approved. In fact, some churches do not have—and even reject the idea of—formal doctrinal statements. However, those churches share beliefs that function in much the same way as formal statements. Informal doctrines usually help a congregation clarify its more formal affirmations. However, informal doctrine can sometimes be pernicious, especially when it is never acknowledged and, hence, is never the object of doctrinal criticism.

The preacher's jobs include helping the congregation identify the formal doctrines of the church and helping the congregation discover how systematic theology unfolds these doctrines for the present. The preacher also must help the congregation name the informal doctrines that are a part of its life and to lead the congregation in reflecting critically on them. Clearly, then, a pastor needs not only to preach doctrine, but also to bring the fuller work of systematic theology into the pulpit.

THEOLOGICAL CRITERIA FOR
THE EVERYDAY LIFE OF THE CHURCH

Systematic theology relates to the everyday life of the church, and I am indebted to Clark M. Williamson, Dean of Christian Theological Seminary, for his helpful perspective on this relationship. Williamson notes that the vocation of the church is to make the Christian witness. The church makes this witness through everything that happens in its life—through preaching, worship, teaching, relationships among members, congregational spending, and actions beyond the congregation. Systematic theology helps the church reflect critically on its witness from the perspective of the historical context in which the church finds itself.[7]

Williamson proposes that the church reflect theologically on its life and the life of the world from the perspective of three criteria:

1. Is the actual life and witness of the church *appropriate* to its deepest beliefs about God and God's purposes in the world?
2. Is the life and witness of the church *intelligible*? That is, can we understand it? Does the life and witness of the church cohere logically with the core of Christian belief? Does it make sense from the standpoint of the ways in which we understand the world today?
3. Is the life and witness of the church *morally plausible*, that is, are the actions of the church consistent with its deepest convictions concerning God and God's purposes in the world?[8]

The church can reflect on every aspect of its life and witness by using these criteria. Take, for example, our understanding and practice of the breaking of the loaf. Is it appropriate to the congregation's deepest beliefs about God and the world? Intelligible? Morally plausible? What about the way the congregation spends its budget or uses the building? Is the community's witness in the wider world appropriate? Intelligible? Morally plausible? The preacher, of course, can reflect on the content of the sermon from the perspective of these questions. The congregation can put these questions to doctrinal affirmations, as well as asking, for example, Is our theology of the nature and purpose of the church theologically adequate according to these criteria?

When the answers to these questions are "Yes," theology helps the church solidify and amplify its faith and witness. When the answer to any of them is "No," systematic theology helps the church reform its life and witness.

At the same time, we need to recognize that the church may have an insight or an issue that calls into question an aspect of theology. Indeed, systematic theology has a conversational character. In the give-and-take between witness and theological reflection, systematic theology aims to help the Christian community clarify its identity and mission and live out that identity and mission.

These two tasks—making the Christian witness and thinking about it—are not completely separate. As Williamson notes, "We cannot make the Christian witness without thinking about what we are doing, and we cannot think about it without also making it. This distinction is mainly a matter of emphasis."[9]

As an example of the practicality of systematic theology for preaching, consider the pastor who is preparing a sermon on the death penalty. What witness should the church make in this discussion? The church could be categorically opposed to the death penalty, could advocate the limited use of the death penalty, or could regard the death penalty as routine punishment for certain crimes. The Bible offers mixed guidance on this subject. On the one hand, one can cite occasional biblical texts and principles that ruminate against taking life. On the other hand, biblical Israel sometimes practiced the death penalty. And the earliest churches, while not having the authority to engage in capital punishment, were part of the Roman world, in which criminals were executed. Yet the earliest Christian literature does not object directly to these acts. Moreover, while we can extrapolate objections to the death penalty by analogy from certain teachings of Jesus and from vectors of Paul's theology, these materials do not specifically address the death penalty. Furthermore, the history of the church's witness on this subject is ambiguous. While we can cite voices that object to the death penalty, we must also recognize that the church in the past sometimes put people to death.

Today's preacher needs to help the congregation interpret the theological issues surrounding the death penalty. In order to do so, the preacher cannot rely on a single biblical text, or even a collection of biblical texts, but needs to turn to doctrine and systematic theology. What are God's purposes for human life and community? What is the relationship of the death penalty to those purposes? What is God's role in the giving and taking of life, and what are fitting roles for the human community? The gospel is the dipolar news of God's unconditional love for each and all and God's will for justice for each and all. Justice refers to relationships of love among all people and nature. From this point of view, the Christian community should oppose the death penalty, because putting a person to death denies that God loves the executed person unconditionally, and it ends the possibility that the person can live in relationships of love. Indeed, capital punishment is an unloving action.

THE PREACHER AND INTUITIVE THEOLOGY IN THE CONGREGATION

While preachers often think of systematic theology as the domain of professional systematic theologians, they can be systematic theologians when they make use of systematic theology. Moreover, local pastors contribute to systematic theology when ministerial practice prompts them to theological discoveries that academic systematic theologians have not noticed. Karl Barth, for instance, was pastor of a congregation in Switzerland when his theological renaissance began that eventuated in the thirteen-volume systematic theology *Church Dogmatics*. Reinhold Niebuhr was minister of a congregation in Detroit when several of his key theological insights crystallized. Pastoral listening often helps local ministers become aware of important questions and issues on which they can lead the congregation in creative theological reflection in ways unconsidered by academic theologians.

A number of laypeople who have not had formal theological education have excellent theological sense. Indeed, I am occasionally a guest Bible study leader or preacher in a congregation in which a sensitive layperson has more theological acumen than the seminary-educated pastor.

Interpreters of the church often speak of today's congregations as theologically illiterate. And it is true that few Christian communities today can adequately articulate the basic content of Christian faith or have a clear method for reflecting on their beliefs and witness. However, the fact that a congregation cannot speak in a systematic way about theological concerns does not mean that the congregation is theologically inert. Although a congregation may not be able to state formally its core convictions, such convictions typically exist in a congregation informally, and even intuitively.

For example, when my spouse and I were co-pastors in Nebraska, one of our church members made a statement of stunning theological penetration during a board meeting. Other members of the board immediately nodded their heads in agreement, and the board member's observation turned the discussion in a very constructive direction. After the meeting I asked the member what had led her to that bold declaration. She replied, "I just feel that way." Other board members who were with us nodded in agreement.

With a little prompting, she put together a rationale based on bits and pieces of the Bible, our denomination's customs at the Table, and memories of sermons of preachers in the past. When she finished, I offered the equivalent of a paragraph of systematic theology to interpret her position, and her face lit up. "Sure. That's it." She could not articulate her theology, but tacit theological values were at work in her worldview.

Theology at the level of intuition results from at least four factors. The first and most important is God's omnipresence and its often unspoken effects. People intuit God's presence and movement. They apprehend the divine at the level of feeling without becoming fully conscious. In the process, they develop a theological intuition that informs their thoughts and actions but which they have not enunciated.

Second, Christian practice often orients the self to perceive the world along Christian lines. As I explain more fully in chapter 2, Christian practice is the congregation's intentional, repeated activities that are designed to encourage Christian identity and behavior. Practices shape our worldviews, sometimes without our conscious awareness. The board member in our congregation in Nebraska gave evidence of being affected by Christian practice when she spoke of how our denomination's custom of the weekly breaking of the loaf had influenced her perspective on an issue.

Third, studies in mental operation reveal that some people are highly deductive, systematic, linear in thought, and mathematically precise in thought and speech. By contrast, other people are more inductive, associative, intuitive, and given to metaphor, image, and poetry. The members of the latter group (which includes many preachers) have difficulty both stating their own faith systematically and entering into the systematic statements of others.

Fourth, pastors seldom help the congregation verbalize their faith in a systematic way. Intuition remains powerful but unconscious and unspoken.

The difficulty with theology that remains tacit is that congregations have great difficulty reflecting critically on it. Much of the informal and intuitive theology at work in congregations coheres with normative Christian vision. People have a gut sense of a God of unconditional love and for making decisions in behalf of justice. However, to be candid, some of the informal and intuitive values that are at work in congregations are sub-Christian, even anti-Christian. Racism, for example, often operates unconsciously.

Part of the theological task of the sermon is to name the actual theology, including intuitive elements, that operate at the center of the congregation's life. Toward this end, the pastor needs to listen carefully to the congregation in order to enumerate what the congregation actually believes about God, Jesus Christ, the Holy Spirit, the church, and the world. Another part of the theological task of the sermon is to lead the community in reflecting on those elements. When a congregation is able to articulate its actual convictions, it can evaluate them and, as necessary, amplify, extend, or correct them.

Systematic theology is a significant pastoral resource for the preacher as it provides a lens through which to interpret the life of the Christian community and the world. The overarching convictions that come to clarity in systematic theology help the preacher make sense of biblical passages, personal situations in the lives of listeners, developments in the Christian community, and circumstances in the wider world.

2

Why the Church Needs
Systematic Theology
in Preaching Today

Systematic theology is always in season. Without a strong theological heart, a congregation is likely to be "tossed to and fro and blown about by every wind of doctrine, by people's trickery, by their craftiness in deceitful scheming" (Eph. 4:14). The congregation with a vibrant theology speaks the truth in love so that the community "grows up in every way into [the one] who is the head, into Christ" (Eph. 4:15). Such a congregation is strong not only in its internal life, but also in its witness in the face of the principalities and powers that oppress, exploit, and violate the world (Eph. 6:10–17). In short, theology helps the congregation recognize and respond to the presence of the living God.

There are six reasons why preaching needs to give systematic theology a high profile today:

1. Systematic theology in preaching helps appropriately shape Christian community for today.
2. Many people today are hungry for the holistic interpretation of life that systematic theology offers.
3. Preaching systematic theology helps the church make sense of diverse theological claims.
4. Preaching out of systematic theology helps pastor and congregation relate to the pluralism of postmodernity.
5. Explicit theology in sermons is an antidote for theological illiteracy.
6. Systematic theology helps the preacher honor the integrity of elements of the Bible and Christian tradition.

SHAPING CHRISTIAN COMMUNITY

Theological conviction is the heart of Christian community and shapes the life and witness of the community. Systematic theology leads the church in defining what we believe about God, Jesus Christ, the Spirit, the world, and the church, and in determining how to embody these beliefs. These beliefs define the Christian community as well as the relationship of the Christian community to the larger culture. Our theological beliefs determine the attitudes, behaviors, policies, and feelings that the church regards as acceptable and not acceptable. Theological affirmations guide the church toward the stands that it takes (or does not take) in its internal affairs and in public life.

Christopher Morse, professor of systematic theology at Union Theological Seminary in New York, points out that the church is also defined by what we do not believe.[1] Every affirmation the church makes simultaneously also implies what the church cannot believe or cannot do. When, for instance, the church says yes to the idea that the earth and its resources are the gift of a gracious God to support the whole human family (and other forms of life), it must also say no to the exploitation of the earth for the benefit of a few people and to the neglect of others. Theology helps the church distill its guiding convictions and their consequences in feeling and behavior.

Systematic theology leads the church in naming norms by which to gauge the things that are essential and nonessential, acceptable and unacceptable, in the Christian house. Theology helps the preacher and the church specify the things to which it says yes and no.

In the current rediscovery of Christian practice, there is an emphasis on the complexity of the ways in which persons and communities develop in faith. Of course, what we say we believe influences what we actually believe and feel as well as how we act, but how we act also influences what we believe and feel. Those in the area of Christian practice use the term "practice" to designate an intentional activity in which the church engages over time to help develop Christian identity and behavior.[2] A practice shapes thinking, feeling, and behaving. Practices yield a way of life.

Systematic theology helps the church reflect on the degree to which the practices of the church adequately embody our most penetrating understanding of God and Christian life and witness. At the same time, theology and practice relate dialectically. Christian practice raises the question of whether systematic theology represents God and the Christian life as fully and accurately as is necessary.

For instance, worship each week is a practice in which the church liturgically represents its understanding of God, God's relationship with the world, and the human response to the divine purposes. "We use the familiar elements of everyday life—food, water, oil, embrace, word—to proclaim and celebrate what God is doing in the world and in our lives."[3] What we say and do in miniature in the highly symbolic language and actions of worship patterns us to engage in similar expressions of language and action in a larger way in the everyday world. We praise God as the author and sustainer of life. We confess our complicity in the brokenness of the world. We listen to scripture and sermon to remember God's continuing faithfulness and to figure out how we can fulfill the divine purposes in our social settings. We place offerings on the Table to represent our offering of ourselves to God in the home, on the job, and at play. We receive the gift of bread and cup as demonstration that God is always with us, and as norm for our own hospitality and willingness to work for the well-being of the neighbor.

To continue the preceding example, systematic theology helps the preacher think critically about what the church says and does in worship. Do the hymns represent the character of God in a way that is consistent with optimum theological vision? Do the readings from the Bible and the sermon speak of God's activity in the world in a way that the preacher and congregation can fully endorse? Does the church's practice of hospitality at the sacred meal act out the inclusiveness of divine love? At the same time, the worship of the church presses the preacher and theologian to consider whether their theological formulations are sufficient. For example, is the inclusivity and graciousness of God demonstrated at the breaking of the loaf also represented in the way in which the preacher speaks of God and in the church's doctrinal formulations?

Sometimes we say we believe one thing when our behavior indicates that we believe something else. When this happens, the preacher can use systematic theology to lead the church to reflect on the degree to which its actions are continuous and discontinuous with what it says it believes. Theology helps the preacher disclose contradictions between belief and behavior and to call for reform that brings belief and behavior into consistency.

Systematic theology should play a crucial role in helping shape Christian community today. In North America the church has often had difficulty maintaining its distinctive Christian identity and behavior. The long-established denominations—such as the Episcopal Church, the Christian Church (Disciples of Christ), the Presbyterian Church (U.S.A.), the Roman Catholic Church, the United Methodist Church, the United Church of Christ—have become closely identified with North American culture and values.[4] This assimilation of culture by Christianity is a central cause of the decline in membership and institutional health in the long-established denominations; many people conclude that participating in the church adds nothing to their lives that they do not get elsewhere. Consequently, they have no reason to stay in the church.[5] Furthermore, some Christians presume that God wills capitalism, nationalism, class superiority, and even racism. In so doing, they drift into idolatry, injustice, and violence. Indeed, some churches even create ideologies to support such endeavors.

A robust systematic theology helps the preacher monitor the relationship between the church and the culture so that the church can maintain its distinctive witness to the purposes of God for the world. The church does not need to be different for the sake of being different, but it does need a critical relationship with the culture so that its particular voice is not stifled by accommodation to the culture. The church is then in a position both to critique aspects of the culture that deny the gospel as well as to reinforce movements in the culture that deny the gospel and distort the divine purposes.[6]

A congregation tends to pattern itself after the theological vision at the center of its life. A congregation whose doctrine is rigid, exclusive, and legalistic, and whose works are righteous tends to manifest those qualities in its own life and to call for them in the wider world. A congregation whose doctrine is alive, inclusive, generous, and gracious tends to embody those characteristics in its life and to work for a similar world.

A HUNGER FOR SYSTEMATIC THEOLOGY

You may read this subheading and think, "No one in my congregation asks me questions about systematic theology." While it is true that laypeople seldom ask questions in the technical language of systematic theology, many laypeople long to understand life in a meaningful way. They want to know explicitly and intuitively how to make sense of existence. People sometimes ask these questions in conventional religious language. "When I pray, I would like to know what I can count on." At other times, these questions are expressed in language that is not explicitly associated with religion but that reveals a religious concern. My spouse and I currently have four teenagers who are all variously asking, "What am I going to do with my life?" They want to know more than, "What kind of job am I going to get?" They want to know who they are and how they can express their real identities in their life activities.

The influential cultural anthropologist Clifford Geertz explains that the fundamental purpose of religion is to help people interpret life. A religion, he notes, is "(1) a system of symbols which acts to (2) establish powerful, pervasive, and long-lasting moods and motivations in [human beings] by (3) formulating conceptions of a general order of existence and (4) clothing these conceptions with such an aura of factuality that (5) the moods and motivations seem uniquely realistic."[7] The oldest and most important function of religion is to offer a holistic interpretation that shows how the various pieces of life fit together in such a way as to allow the human community to feel that existence is purposeful and that life is not going to be overwhelmed by chaos.

Religion provides orientation and meaning in the midst of a world that is often threatening and meaningless. Even when religion does not eliminate danger, it provides perspectives that allow human beings to make their way through the vicissitudes of the world. Religion uses symbols (words as well as symbolic actions, materials, and places) to make long-lasting intellectual sense of the world, and it charges that sense with emotional power. Religion speaks of life in ways that the community finds believable and that are confirmed in its experience. Religion proffers the meaning of time and space, and locates the human community in them. Religion shows how life is ordered in such a way that it will not be overcome by the threat of chaos. In sum, religion makes sense of life.

Systematic theology contributes directly to this purpose by offering a holistic interpretation of life from a Christian perspective. It does this by identifying the specific categories that are essential to Christian understanding of the world and by showing how they relate with one another. For instance, who is God and how does God relate with the world? What is the nature of the world? What does God do? What can we count on God to do? What do we need to do? What are optimum goals of human community, and what is necessary for people to move toward them? One of the most existentially important functions of systematic theology is to help the congregation make sense of seemingly random experiences of threat, pain, and chaos. The preacher can explicitly draw on systematic theology in the sermon to unfold the meaning of life.

In doing this, theology helps the sermon respond to two of the deepest existential human questions. Who are we? What are we to do? Systematic theology helps preachers respond to the first question by locating our finite individual and communal lives in relationship with the One who is transcendent and infinite. Theology helps us respond to the second question by identifying the qualities of life that issue from our answer to the first question. Values generate behavior; behavior enacts values.

SORTING THROUGH DIVERSE
THEOLOGICAL CLAIMS

The church is becoming more and more aware of the diversity of voices in the Bible, in Christian tradition, and in the contemporary church. On the one hand, this discovery is liberating. The very fact of differing points of view in the tradition reminds us that the church is not imprisoned by the doctrinal formulations of previous generations but is a living community that constantly thinks about credible ways to understand its faith that take account of fresh contexts and, at the same time, thinks about ways to interpret our contemporary context from the standpoint of Christian tradition.

Christian tradition is not simply a deposit of unchangeable doctrine. The word "tradition" is from the Latin verb *traditio*, which would be rendered "traditioning." The Christian tradition is less a deposit that is transferred from the vaults of faith from one generation to another, and more the record of the process of coming to understandings of God, Jesus Christ, the Holy Spirit, the church, and the world for each new era. Furthermore, in the diversity of scripture and the Christian past we find voices that prompt the church today to question the adequacy of current formulations.

On the other hand, the diversity of the Bible and Christian tradition raises questions. What is the relationship of these voices with one another? Which voices does the Christian community regard as authoritative, and why? What does the church do when it comes eyeball to eyeball with a thought, feeling, or action from Christian tradition that is troubling theologically or morally?

For instance, the Second Testament contains diverse understandings of Jesus Christ. Several of these understandings contain elements that overlap, but I will portray them starkly to call attention to their distinctiveness: For Mark, Jesus is the apocalyptic redeemer who announces the imminent apocalypse that will fully manifest of the realm of God. Mark depicts many Jewish leaders and institutions to be possessed by Satan. For

Matthew, Jesus is a rabbi, on the model of a Pharisee, who instructs the disciples in how to live faithfully as a Torah-observant community given the expectation of the imminent end of this world. By contrast, the Fourth Gospel criticizes apocalypticism (e.g., John 11:24–27) but also depicts Jesus as the word become flesh who was with God at the creation of the world, and who has come from the heavenly realm to reveal God, life, truth, freedom, light, and the way to the heaven in the midst of this world of death, falsehood, slavery, and darkness. In the early Christian sermon to the Hebrews, Jesus is a high priest after the order of Melchizedek who mediates a new and better covenant than the one that God made with Israel. The Bible climaxes its pictures of Jesus Christ in the book of Revelation by envisioning Jesus as the sovereign of the cosmos. Enthroned with God, Jesus is the ruler of the rulers of the earth. Although idolatrous, unjust, and violent Rome may appear to control the earth at present, the reader quickly learns that Rome's dominion is temporary for Jesus already sits at the right hand of God and will soon destroy Rome (an agent of Satan) and will fully manifest the divine rule on the earth.

The different perspectives on Jesus in the Second Testament emerged from communities that were in different theological and social locations. While we can understand why each community articulated its particular perception of Jesus Christ in view of its circumstance, today's church cannot simply add together these different points of view (and others that developed in Christian history after the Bible was written) to create a Christology. Such an approach makes absolute the claims of previous generations, ignores the contributions our context might make to Christology, and results in a Christology containing contradictory elements.

Systematic theology helps the preacher sum up her or his perception of Jesus Christ today in a way that maintains continuity with the Bible and Christian tradition but reconsiders them for our time. Systematic theology in the sermon will dialogue with historic understandings of Jesus Christ and will bring promising aspects of them into the church's contemporary formulation. Along the way, historical and systematic theology can help the church understand why particular christo-logical themes emerged in particular periods, but the larger work of theology is to help the preacher envision a Christology that serves God in our time similarly to the ways in which previous Christologies served their times.

Theology similarly helps the preacher understand the multiple forms of diversity in Christian community. The church manifests differences not only in doctrine and other theological claims but also in Christian practices within the community, as well as in mission in the larger world. Differences among churches on such matters can be substantial, and can result in painful polarization. For instance, as I write, the church is divided over the issue of whether a person must become a Christian in order to be saved or whether all persons are saved. Relatively few Christians have a self-conscious (or even intuitive) theological method that allows them to think through the issue. Consequently, they toss to and fro in response to sources that they stumble across, ranging from the viewpoints of tele-vangelists, tracts that they pick up in the local mall, Bible texts taken out of context but passed along in folk Christianity, biases passed along as truth in the local coffee shop, scraps of an interview from a philosopher of world religions on public television. In the end, Christians may form their opinions without seriously consulting the Bible, the major voices of Christian tradition, or responsible contemporary sources. The preacher who initiates the congregation into systematic theology and method in the pulpit thus performs a direct pastoral service to the congregation by equipping them to deal with such diversity.

SYSTEMATIC THEOLOGY AND
THE PLURALISM OF POSTMODERNITY

Scholars increasingly use the term "modern" to refer to the worldview that resulted from the Enlightenment. Modern people believed that they could achieve objective, undiluted, universally reliable perception of truth and the world. They sought to achieve such perception on the basis of empirical investigation or coherence with first principles. People could accept something as true if it could be verified by the scientific method (that is, through the senses) or if it agreed with commonly accepted first principles.

As the designation indicates, "postmodernity" is a way of thinking that goes beyond the modern worldview. Postmodern people recognize that all awareness contains interpretive elements; we can never have pure, unadulterated apprehension of the world. Furthermore, postmodernists point out that the scientific method does not always result in conclusions that are valid in every time and place. For example, whereas Newtonian physics were once unquestioned, that approach has now been replaced by quantum physics. Furthermore, not all communities accept the same set of first principles. Indeed, some communities reject the very idea of first principles.[8]

The postmodern ethos is marked by pluralism and relativism. In postmodernity, people are increasingly aware of multiple ways of understanding the world and of conceiving of what is normative. Each particular community posits its own worldview, thus creating a plurality of ways of interpreting the world. Pluralism results in relativity, that is, the recognition that no single way of thinking about the world is absolute or universally accepted, and that all worldviews are partial.

Whereas the melting pot was a common symbol of the goals of the modern world, the salad bowl is a better symbol of the aims of postmodernity. In a melting pot, the individuality of persons and communities dissolves into a homogenous soup, whereas in a salad bowl, the various ingredients retain their individuality but exist alongside one another, and even enhance or support.

On the one hand, people celebrate the pluralism and relativity of postmodernity. The postmodern world honors the particularity of communities. Postmodern folk seek both to respect the individuality of various races and ethnicities, and to refrain from forcing people from differing communities into a homogenous soup. In a postmodern setting, communities are less likely to be subject to arbitrary absolutes. On the other hand, postmodernity raises enervating questions for the Christian community. For example, given the pluralism and relativity of perception in the postmodern era, why should people take seriously the claims of Christianity (especially in comparison to the claims of other religions and the claims of nonreligion)? How does Christianity (and how should Christians) relate to other religions and their adherents? Given the fact that North American culture does not adhere to a commonly accepted set of authorities and values, on what basis can Christians enter into public discussion?

Systematic theology can help the preacher relate to the pluralism of postmodernity in several key ways.[9] It guides the preacher in describing the particularity of the Christian worldview. It helps the preacher compare and contrast Christian ways of perception, feeling, and behavior with those of other communities so that the congregation can identify points at which the Christian worldview is distinctive and points that it shares with others. Recognizing that Christians do not have a monopoly on insight, systematic theology helps the preacher identify sources in the frothing pluralism outside the Christian domain that enrich Christian understanding. Theology construes the world so as to account for God in relationship with pluralism and relativity. Such a theology delineates the sources of authority for the Christian community so that congregations can understand why (and how) they can believe Christian claims. A theologically informed preacher can help the congregation figure out its relationship with other Christian denominations and other religions.

ANTIDOTE FOR THEOLOGICAL ILLITERACY

Most preachers are aware that many people in today's churches are theologically illiterate.[10] That is, they do not have a sufficient formal working familiarity with the main themes of the Bible, Christian tradition, and the core elements of Christian doctrine and systematic theology, nor do they have a clear method for thinking theologically about these matters or about the contemporary life and the world.

As I noted in chapter 1, even when congregations do not have a crisp understanding of what they believe, they usually have an implicit theology. While implicit theology is often consistent with core Christian convictions, it is also often misdirected. For instance, in congregational business meetings, people frequently make decisions on the basis of values that prevail in the world of secular (and sometimes unjust and exploitative) business without reference to satisfactory theological norms, and in the process they lead the congregation toward actions that contradict bedrock Christian belief.

No single element of church life is responsible for widespread contemporary theological illiteracy. Pastors, initiation rites into the congregation, Christian education, stewardship, and mission emphases—all of these share responsibility for leaving the church theologically diminished.

Preaching, too, bears some of the burden for depreciated theological acumen in congregations. After an extensive study of sermons in Presbyterian churches, John S. McClure, a leading scholar of preaching, concludes, "What seems to be missing in Presbyterian preaching now . . . is a consistent and assertive theological message." Indeed, Presbyterian preaching sometimes manifests "inconsistencies and even counteracting theological messages from one sermon to another."[11]

Marsha Witten, a sociologist with theological insight, reviewed sermons preached on the parable of the prodigal child in fifty congregations in long-established denominations. She found a tendency toward accommodation in these sermons, that is, the preachers tend to interpret the story and its theological meaning in ways that "bring them in conformity with the values and behavior of secularity." Witten's observations about how God appears in these sermons represent their overall theological direction. "The scope of discussion is almost entirely reduced to God's functions for the private concerns of human beings. . . . These highlight God's primary functions in providing psychological benefits for individual human beings. . . . God becomes an instrument for the alleviation of the psychological burdens of men and women."[12] In preaching, theology undergoes a "softening" to accommodate to contemporary culture.

Joseph Faulkener, who teaches speech at Pennsylvania State University, studied 206 sermons preached in the Christian Church (Disciples of Christ) and came to a similar conclusion. While he examined sermons on doctrinal matters, he found that "there is more declamation than analytical explanation. The language used to describe the doctrines is almost completely abstract rather than specific. The assumption would appear to be that the congregation knows and understands the doctrine and thus needs simply to be reassured that God does indeed love us, will forgive us, and will save us." But, Faulkener adds, "It is clearly dangerous to assume much doctrinal or even biblical literacy on the part of the congregation."[13]

In response to this earlier trend, David G. Buttrick calls for preaching to take "a turn to theology." The preacher needs not only to articulate "faith in contemporary language and in relation to contemporary structures of thought," but needs to help the congregation learn to "think theologically over events and issues." Preaching can function as "remedial theology" with respect to both content and method as the preacher brings systematic theology directly into the pulpit.[14]

In this scenario, the pastor is not simply the resident theologian who engages in theological reflection for the community. The pastor is a teacher of theology who seeks for the congregation to become a community of theological reflection. When a congregation becomes such a body, the doctrine of the priesthood of all believers comes to life. All Christians become theologians. Indeed, lay participants may exhibit greater theological wisdom than clergy. A congregation that is a *community of theological reflection* will likely have a high degree of ownership of, and energy for, Christian faith, not to mention mission, in the congregation and beyond.

Of course, the various parts of the congregational system must work together to help the congregation become theologically literate. But preaching can play a pivotal role in this renewal, for preaching takes place in the largest regular gathering of the congregation. Week in and week out, the preacher who explicitly brings systematic theology into sermons has opportunities to help the congregation refine its capacity to interpret the world theologically.

HONORING OTHERNESS
IN THE BIBLE AND CHRISTIAN TRADITION

The Jewish philosopher Emmanuel Levinas points out that each person is an other, that is, each is a person with her or his own identity and integrity. Consequently, we can never know an other fully. The other has the capacity to enrich my experience by adding dimensions of her or his otherness to my world, by calling into question things that I take for granted, by offering me alternative ways of thinking and acting, by forcing me to think more deeply about myself and my relationship with others and the world.[15]

However, Levinas laments that Western culture tends to reduce otherness to sameness with us in order to reduce the risk and potential change that results from encounters with an other.[16] I tend to project my own preferences onto other individuals. A community tends to assume that other communities share the same values and ethics.

A biblical text or an element of Christian tradition is also an other, that is, an entity with its own identity and integrity. Recent scholarship of the Bible and Christian history notes that biblical and other Christian texts are multivalent in meaning; the full dimensions of meaning in a passage can seldom be captured in a single reading. Fresh circumstances or fresh data prompt us to perceive texts in fresh ways. Scholars rightly warn us against the reductionistic fallacy of thinking that we can deduce *the* meaning of a passage. Contemporary exegesis agrees that we should hear a passage in ways that are consistent with how it could have been heard by early communities, that is, in its historical, literary, rhetorical, and theological contexts in antiquity. In other words, we should respect the otherness of the text.

Many preachers and congregations have a proclivity to reduce the otherness of a passage from the Bible or Christian tradition to sameness. We tend to see a text as a reflection and confirmation of our already existing ways of thinking, feeling, and acting. In the process, we make the text into an image of preexisting theologies. When this happens, we diminish the capacity of the biblical text or witness from Christian tradition to enrich, call into question, offer alternatives, and prompt us to think more deeply about God and ourselves.

For instance, in Matthew 18:20, Jesus says, "For where two or three are gathered in my name, I am there among them." Typically preachers use this verse to assure people that Jesus is constantly present with them, citing it to comfort people. Unfortunately, this sentiment misrepresents the meaning of the verse in its context. Matthew 18:15–20 instructs the church in how to deal with members of the church who violate the community by disrupting the church's witness to the realm of God. The church is to take a series of steps (going to the person individually, then with others) to encourage such persons to bring their attitudes and behavior into conformity with the reign of God. If the recalcitrant persons do not, the church is to expel them from the community. So, Matthew 18:20 actually promises the church that the risen Jesus is present and working through community processes of church discipline and excommunication. This text is a distinctive other to many Christians in the long-established denominations who are uncomfortable with the idea of excommunication. Hence, they overlook the larger Matthean context and fasten on the truncated meaning above.

Systematic theology allows the church to hear this passage in its Matthean otherness without forcing the text into the sameness of conventional piety. At the level of general conviction (and not dependent simply on Matthew 18:20), theology assures the congregation that Jesus is, indeed, constantly present in all life circumstances. The passage contributes to, but does not singularly determine, the church's theological reflection on the question of whether persons who violate the realm of God should continue in the Christian community.

Systematic theology encourages the preacher to enter into open and honest conversation with biblical texts and other elements of Christian tradition as a part of exploring what we really do (and do not) believe. A preacher with a well-defined systematic theology does not have to violate the integrity of a passage from the Bible or an aspect of Christian tradition by reading his or her own theology into the text to find the text useful in preaching.[17] Even when an other from the Bible or Christian past makes the preacher and congregation uncomfortable, the conversation around that discomfort can help the church clarify what we can believe and what we should do. Indeed, such a conversation may encourage preacher and congregation to fresh consideration or reconsideration of the text or topic.

When I float the idea of preaching systematic theology with preachers, someone nearly always says, "But the congregation will be bored to death." However, Lyle Schaller, who studies congregational life, notices that congregations have a remarkable capacity to follow long and complex sermons when the content makes a vital connection with the experience of the congregation, when the language of the sermon is vivid, when the message moves so that the congregation can easily follow it, and when the preacher embodies the sermon in an engaging way.[18] This finding coheres with the observation above that many people today are hungry for systematic theology. The sermon that correlates the hunger of the congregation with the rich sustenance of systematic theology presented creatively can nourish the understanding of the congregation, strengthen the heart of the community, and swell the glory the people give to God.

3

Biblical Preaching through the Lens of Systematic Theology

Most preaching in the long-established denominations today originates with the Bible. The preacher begins with a biblical text and seeks to help the congregation understand how encounter with the passage helps the community become more deeply aware of, and responsive to, the divine presence and purposes.[1] Many pastors follow a lectionary as the basis for their sermons, but pastors who do not subscribe to a lectionary still develop sermons that originate with the Bible.

In many respects, this emphasis on the Bible is welcome.[2] However, as the previous chapters made clear, the Bible is not the only source or statement of convictions at the core of Christian identity. Indeed, individual passages from the Bible do not always cohere with one another or represent the heart of Christian vision. Christian convictions transcend particular biblical passages and are summarized in the fuller world of systematic theology. Yet, despite the importance of theology, contemporary preaching often gives it a low profile. Theological anemia in the long-established churches suggests that the time is ripe for revitalizing the relationship of the Bible, theology, and preaching.

This chapter urges ministers to preach from the Bible, consciously and critically, through the lens of systematic theology.[3] After recalling that the Bible is a collection of different theologies, I pause over various forms of interference between the

Bible and systematic theology in contemporary preaching. The chapter concludes with a simple conversational model for relating the Bible and systematic theology in the sermon.

THE BIBLE: A COLLECTION OF DIFFERENT THEOLOGIES

The Bible is not a volume of systematic theology. While it contains ideas and images of God, Christ, the Holy Spirit, the church, and the world, the Bible does not sequentially consolidate essential beliefs and practices in the categories or linear format of systematic theology.

The Bible is a collection of different theologies. Different authors and schools of thought in the Bible offer particular interpretations of the divine presence, purposes, and modes of operation.[4] The theological perspectives of the biblical writers are expressed in a variety of genres, ranging from multiple kinds of narratives through various forms of poetry and proverbs to rhetorical styles adapted from other people in antiquity. From each theological perspective in the Bible, we could extrapolate a systematic summary of theological views by category, but, of course, something would be lost in the transition from narrative, poetry, or proverb to propositional summary. Furthermore, sequential, categorical thinking of the kind represented in systematic theology is not indigenous to the Semitic mind and heart.

To be sure, the theological perspectives in the Bible share certain foundational principles. However, despite important theological affinities, the different theological households offer different perspectives on God, on how we know God, and on the possibilities for human life and the natural world.

This brief overview reminds us that we never simply "preach the Bible," for the Bible is not a singular, unified theological document. When we preach from a particular biblical passage, we are working with a distinct theological perspective within the Bible as refracted through the particular text.

We may speak broadly of eight major theological classifications that can be found in the literature of the Bible [see the list, below]. We can identify some of these perspectives easily because distinct books are devoted to them, such as the Deuteronomic theology. Other theologies are less easily identified. For example, the older Elohist and the Yahwistic theologies are now integrated into the more recent Deuteronomic and priestly writings. In the Bible itself, then, theologians from one generation or perspective interpret the perspectives of others, adding to and subtracting from the tradition and also redirecting it.

Some of you may be surprised that I designate all of these classifications by names that have Jewish associations. I do this because earliest Christianity was a movement within Judaism, and was in close (if frequently conflicted) relationship with Judaism through most of the period in which the Second Testament came to expression.[5] The earliest Christians largely interpreted Jesus Christ and the early Christian mission through theological categories of Judaism, augmented with concepts from the wider Hellenistic world.

I speak of these theological classifications as if they are distinct. However, their motifs often interact. The eight perspectives follow, along with some of their primary characteristics—for example, where the material is found in the Bible, its historical context, how the community knows God, its theological core, the divine purpose for the human community and nature, groups whose social power is legitimated by the theological position, and other distinctive features. While the voices of the Elohist and the Yahwist have now been subsumed in materials edited by the Deuteronomists and the priestly theologians, I mention them separately because their perspectives are still identifiable, and their presence in this list reminds us that theological pluralism was a fact in Israel from early days. The Elohistic, Yahwistic, Deuteronomic, priestly, and apocalyptic theologies all have the notion of covenant at their theological core. Obedience to the stipulations of the covenant result in blessing while disobedience results in curse. However, not all the theologians below share this viewpoint.

Elohists. The Elohistic theology is embedded largely in Genesis, Exodus, and Numbers. We call these authors "Elohists" because Elohim is the name they use most frequently for God. The Elohists wrote in northern Israel in about 850 B.C.E. Their goal was to help consolidate the formation of the northern monarchy. Elohim is so transcendent in this literature that we know the divine mainly through intermediaries such as Moses (the quintessential interpreter of the divine). This literature shows little interest in the creation of the world but establishes community confidence on the basis of God's care of the ancestral families and the deliverance from Egypt.

Yahwists. The Yahwistic theology is embedded in texts in Genesis and Exodus and occasional other documents. We call the writers "Yahwists" because YHWH is their name for God. Yahwists wrote from about 1000 to 922 B.C.E. when the former tribal confederacy, at Shiloh, was consolidating into a monarchy with a strong central government in Jerusalem. This theology calls attention to YHWH as the creator of the world. That claim is the foundation of the Yahwist's confidence that God controls history and purposes to bless the whole human family using Israel as the means of blessing. We know God through divine actions in history. Yahwistic theology legitimates both the monarchy and the transfer of power from Shiloh to Jerusalem. During this time, the community was in danger of accommodating its distinctive faith to pagan practices. Hence, the Yahwists call the people to repent from disobedience and to turn toward YHWH for covenantal blessing.

Deuteronomists. The Deuteronomic theology is found especially in the books beginning with Deuteronomy and extending through 2 Kings. Protodeuteronomism (theological ideas that contain the seeds of Deuteronomic theology but are not yet fully developed Deuteronomism) underlies Amos, Hosea, Isaiah 1–39, Jeremiah, Micah, and Zephaniah. This world of thought came to expression from 700 to 550 B.C.E., before and during the exile. The Deuteronomist supports the Davidic monarchy and assumes that the postexilic government will be Davidic. The community knows God through study. The people are to study the traditions of the community to confront the fate of those who disobey the covenant (and fall under curse) and to discern the path to obedience and blessing. The tradition is contemporized: the community feels the power that operated in the past still operating, as in the expression, "When *we* were slaves in Egypt . . ."

Priests. The priests gave much of the books of Genesis through Numbers their present shape, as well as 1 and 2 Chronicles, Ezra, Nehemiah, Isaiah 40–55, Ezekiel, Haggai, Zechariah 1–8, Obadiah, Joel, Malachi, and a number of the Psalms. Writing prior to and during the exile (600–500 B.C.E.), the priests stress right worship as the key to community holiness and blessing. Whereas the Deuteronomists identified the continuation of the Davidic monarchy as God's plan for the future, the priests see the people becoming a community of priests who embody holiness and who are a light to the nations. Their emphasis on worship legitimates the priestly writers' social power; they professed their interpretation of Torah through worship. The liturgical style of Genesis 1 (given its present shape by the priestly community) evokes the atmosphere of worship over the whole telling of the Jewish story and suggests that worship is a part of the very fabric of creation.

Wisdom. Wisdom is found in Proverbs, Ecclesiastes, Job, some of the Psalms, in occasional passages in the prophets, as well as in Wisdom of Solomon and Sirach (also known as Ben Sira, Ecclesiasticus) and in occasional materials in the Second Testament. Much (not all) wisdom literature emerged from the upper class, people who were largely satisfied with life and sought principles that would enable the continuation of the status quo. The wisdom writers believe that God created the world in such a way that we can learn of God through experience, and, hence we learn of God's purposes for life through our observations and experiences.

God aims for human begins to become wise, that is, to discover the patterns of thinking, feeling, and acting that are in harmony with God's principles and that lead to a good life in community. Some sages, however (e.g., Ecclesiastes), reflect on experience and come to a pessimistic view of life. The idea of covenant is less important in wisdom thinking. Some wisdom thinkers (e.g., Job) question the adequacy of the covenantal formula that obedience leads to blessing and disobedience results in curse. The sages sometimes personify wisdom as a woman.

Apocalypticism. We find protoapocalyptic ideas (themes that anticipate apocalypticism but that are not fully developed apocalyptic theology) in Isaiah 56–66 and Zechariah 9–12. Fully developed apocalyptic theology came to expression in 300 B.C.E. and lasted through 200 C.E. in Daniel 7–12 and other Jewish writings that are not found in the protestant canon. The best known of these writings are 2 Esdras, *Enoch*, 2 Baruch, and the Testaments of the Twelve Patriarchs. Apocalypticism is the basic framework of the writings of Paul, Mark, Matthew, Luke–Acts, and the book of Revelation. This literature comes from people who felt marginalized and threatened and who believed they were living at the end of the old world and the beginning of the new. For Christians, Jesus Christ is the agent whom God uses to effect the transition from the old eon to the new. Whereas the theologies mentioned so far presume that the purposes of God will be fulfilled within this world, apocalypticism believes that God will destroy the present broken world and replace it with a new one in which all peoples and nature dwell together in peace, justice, and abundance. The community knows these things because God reveals them, frequently in highly imagistic and symbolic apocalyptic visions.

Hellenistic Judaism. The literature of Hellenistic Judaism (e.g., Wisdom of Solomon, Sirach, 4 Maccabees, Gospel and letters of John, Hebrews; the Pastoral and Petrine letters), which began c. 300 B.C.E., is diverse, but its authors shared a common concern—to interpret Hellenistic philosophy (and other traditions) from the perspective of Judaism and Christianity, and vice versa. These theologians aimed to help their communities maintain faithful Jewish or Christian identity while adapting some of their beliefs to Hellenism. For example, Hellenistic philosophers sometimes spoke of the "logos" as the rational principle of existence. Some Hellenistic Jewish thinkers correlated this notion with that of wisdom. In contrast to the apocalyptic theologians, Hellenistic Jewish theologians tended to share the view that God animates people to an abundant or virtuous life in this world. For Christians, Jesus is the means whereby people know God fully and through whom people are animated. Some Hellenistic Jewish literature moves in the direction of a material/nonmaterial duality.

Voices that are hard to classify. The materials in this category represent not a distinct group but rather a collection of voices that do not fit in a single category. Some are quite brief (e.g., God attempts to kill Moses in Exod. 4:26), while others are longer (e.g., Jonah, Ruth, Esther). This collection of materials epitomizes the plurality of theologies in the worlds of Judaism and Christianity. The preacher needs to honor each of these documents and determine the context, purpose, and theology of each voice.

While the books and passages within each of these eight classifications share certain general characteristics, each is also distinct. When working with individual authors, books, or passages, preachers should honor the particularity of each part of the Bible, and should not reduce an author, a book, or a passage to just the representation of a category. For instance, while both Mark and Luke–Acts anticipate an apocalyptic cataclysm, Mark believes that day is in the immediate future while Luke–Acts prepares the community for a delay. Particular writers, books, or passages often give their own interpretations to themes within the classification, or integrate concerns from other classifications. The Gospel of Matthew, for example, is basically apocalyptic but contains wisdom sayings.

INTERFERENCE AMONG BIBLE, SYSTEMATIC THEOLOGY, AND PREACHING

The Bible's theological pluralism raises a significant question for the preacher: What is the relationship of the Bible's theologies to the theology of the contemporary community? Do we preach the theology of the text? By that I mean, in the sermon do we assume that the congregation should assent to the theology of the text that we are preaching? Or do we relate to the text in some other way? I posit a simple conversational model in response to this question in the next section, but first I pause to note five kinds, or examples, of interference that can occur when the preacher tries to tie together the Bible, systematic theology, and the sermon.

1. Disregarding the theological pluralism of the Bible. An example: Each Sunday, the pastor recommends the theology of the text to the congregation. That theology becomes the operative theology for the day without reference to other theological options. When preaching out of a Deuteronomic text, the preacher commends a Deuteronomic view of how the community knows God and its understanding of the divine purpose for the human community. The sermon presupposes the covenantal notion so prominent in the Deuteronomic history that obedience begets blessing while disobedience begets a curse. Then, a few weeks later, in a sermon on a text from the wisdom tradition, the preacher advocates wisdom perspectives on how we know God and on the divine purpose for life. The problem is that a sermon that reproduces the wisdom theology of Job will almost inherently be in conflict with one that incorporates Deuteronomy's straightforward assertion of the relationship between blessing and cursing. The congregation hears each voice from the Bible but has little help in sorting through the theological differences among them.

This approach to preaching has obvious problems. Although the various theologies of the Bible share core convictions, they also contain differing and even contradictory elements. When the preacher skips week by week from one biblical theology to another, the congregation does not know how to resolve the differences between the theologies or what to believe concerning the nature of God or God's purposes in the world, or how it should respond. Which is true—Deuteronomy or Job? For me, as for most pastors I know, the answer is, "Neither Deuteronomy nor Job contains a theological vision that is full enough for the present day. They do not take into account the centuries of reflection that have enriched the church in the intervening years." Nor can I casually overcome the gap between their theologies and mine by saying blandly, "They need each other," and then looking for a middle way between them. To be sure, my theology draws on elements of Deuteronomy and Job, but brings them into a larger relationship than simply patching them together.

Furthermore, an unreflective preacher who simply reproduces the theology of a passage from the Bible could actually say something in the sermon that goes against the grain of his or her core convictions. At the beginning of a preaching course, the students summarized their core theological convictions so that the class could compare the theology of their sermons with their stated theologies. One of the students identified one of her core theological convictions as God's omnipresence, that is, the idea that God is present in every moment of every day. But when she, in a sermon, raised the question posed by Psalm 88 (and several other Psalms)—"O [God], why do you cast me off? Why do you hide your face from me?"—she muddled around asking, "Why does God turn away from us sometimes?" After the sermon, I asked her, "Weren't you aware of the contradiction between what you really believe and what you said?" The student got a befuddled look and replied, "Well, no . . . I didn't notice."

Disregarding the pluralism of the Bible can also have the effect of subtly communicating to the congregation the idea that the theological position of the text is the only position on an issue. This effect can severely limit a community's theological reflection, especially when the Bible and the wider tradition of the church contain multiple viewpoints. To take an obvious example, a number of passages in the Bible presume the validity of holy war. Some passages portray God authorizing capital pun-ishment. However, the Bible—and the history of the church—contains other voices that militate against capital punishment.

2. Projecting your own theology directly into the text with-out regard for the theology of the text itself. Sometimes called eisegesis, here, the preacher speaks as if the text says what the preacher's theology wants it to say even when the text says something else.

Preachers who are trained in critical biblical scholarship can often spot such interpretive moves on the part of others. For instance, recently a radio preacher interpreted the parable of the talents (Matt. 24:14–30) as Jesus' admonition to work hard so that we can be financially successful. I have also heard that parable used to justify capitalism. The exegetically alert preacher, of course, recognizes immediately that such eiseget-ical interpretations are imported to the text from conventional North American capitalist values. In fact, the parable actually calls the church to multiply its witness to the realm of God even in the face of difficulty. Of course, the realm of God ends the striving for money, because God provides abundantly for all. Thus, the popular interpretation turns the parable inside out.

However, even pastors who are committed to the critical interpretation of the Bible can unintentionally read their own theology into biblical passages. Most pastors, for instance, want to think of Jesus as inviting all people to recognize the realm of God and to participate in its movement. Moreover, we all like to think of the parables as the stories that best illuminate this realm and invite people into it. So, when they encounter a para-ble in the Gospel of Mark, they assure their congregations that parables are intended to clarify Jesus' announcement that the realm of God is already at work among us. In the Second Gospel, however, the opposite meaning pertains. According to Mark 4:10–13, during the earthly ministry of Jesus, the para-bles were intended to obscure Jesus' message to those who were outside Jesus' circle. Moreover, Jesus had to explain the other-wise hidden meaning of the parables to his own hearers or they did not understand them (e.g., Mark 4:13–20, 33–34). This reflects the frequent notion in apocalyptic theology that God hides the fact that the apocalyptic transformation of history is under way until the time that God chooses to reveal it to all people. Today's preacher may not be comfortable with that dimension of apocalyptic theology, but the preacher cannot make that theology other than what it is.

Reading one's own theology into a text violates the integrity of the text. It also misrepresents the text by making it appear to say something it does not. Listeners come away thinking they have heard the Bible when, in fact, they have heard the preacher's misrepresentation of the Bible.

3. Using scripture to support a theological point without reference to the historical, literary, or theological contexts of the passage. During Lent, for example, I occasionally hear a sermon or a series of sermons on the doctrine of the death of Jesus in which the preacher refers in proof-text fashion to meanings of that death. While I have never heard all of the following interpretations in one sermon, I have heard several of them piled on top of one another in a single homily. Usually they occur in a sermon that does not have an overarching theological interpretation to show how they might relate with one another.

In these interpretations the death of Jesus might be viewed as any combination of the following: a martyr death similar to that of a prophet (Matt. 13:57; 23:37), the archetype of the righteous sufferer (Acts 3:14; 7:52; 1 Pet. 3:18), a ransom (Matt. 20:28; Mark 10:45; 1 Pet. 1:18; Rev. 5:9), sacrifice for forgiveness of sin (Matt. 26:28; Heb. 10:12), ending the need for temple sacrifice (Matt. 27:51; Mark 15:38; Heb. 7:27), effecting a renewed covenant (e.g., Matt. 26:26–29), lamb of God who takes away sin (John 2:29; 19:38, 46; 1 Pet. 1:19; Rev. 5:9), moment of exaltation (John 3:14; 12:34); divine mercy seat (Rom. 3:21–26), overcoming the power of sin (Rom. 5:12–21), revelation of the power of God (1 Cor. 1:18–25), self-giving for us that effects various benefits (e.g., Rom. 5:6; 8:3, 32; 1 Cor. 15:3; Gal. 1:4; 2:20; 3:13; 1 Thess. 5:10), means of reconciling Jewish and gentile peoples (Eph. 2:14–18), reconciling the universe (Col. 1:20), expiation (Heb. 2:17; 1 John 2:2; 4:10; cf. Rom. 3:21–26), purification or cleansing (Heb. 1:3; 1 John 1:7), the means of redemption through blood (Heb. 9:12; cf. Rev. 7:14), the servant who suffers in behalf of the community (Acts 3:13; 4:25, 30; 1 Pet. 2:21–25), and agency that destroys the work of the evil one (1 John 3:8).[6]

The fundamental difficulty with this approach is that the preacher acts as if the Bible is a catalogue of theological propositions that the preacher cuts out and pastes into the sermon. This pattern of using the Bible ravages one of the most important principles of contemporary biblical scholarship, namely, that we are to understand *each* book and passage in scripture from the perspective of its *historical, literary, and theological contexts.*

Preachers and theologians who misappropriate scripture in this way engage in a sophisticated form of proof-texting, that is, using a text for one's own purposes without regard for its contexts. Ministers sometimes line up assertions from the eight different theological classifications (summarized above) that articulate very different viewpoints without taking account of the differences, and thereby leave the impression with the congregation that the whole of the Bible is cut from one piece of theological cloth. Ministers sometimes compound the difficulties of this approach by reading their own theologies into some of these shorthand citations from the Bible.

4. Using a particular text as a launching pad into a discussion of a theological concept without making clear that the sermon follows this path. Often, the preacher comes upon a word, image, or idea in the text that prompts him or her to launch into a message that develops an idea at the level of systematic theology without making this transition clear to the congregation. For example, Luke 13:1 recalls some people telling Jesus about Galileans who suffered horrible deaths at the hand of Pilate. Jesus asks those who are with him, "Do you think that because the Galileans suffered in this way they were worse sinners than all other Galileans? No, I tell you." I have heard several preachers use this part of the passage as the launching pad for a sermon that reflects theologically on the relationship of God to suffering. Usually, the preacher seeks to exonerate God from having an active role in causing innocent suffering. While such theology may be quite good in its own right and in another context, the sermon misses entirely the point of the text, revealed in the continuation of Jesus' words. "But unless you repent, you

will all perish just as they did." The Lukan Jesus actually uses the fate of the Galileans as a warning to repent or face a condemnation as painful as the deaths of the innocent Galileans.

This approach leaves people with the mistaken impression that the text deals in a central way with the theological topic that is the focus of the sermon. Dealing with the text takes up time that the preacher could devote to the topic, and sometimes clutters the sermon.

5. Failing to reflect theologically on the biblical passage. Although most introductory textbooks contain a series of steps for putting together a sermon, some of these lists do not include a step that specifically urges the preacher to reflect theologically on the passage.[7] The preacher is seldom asked to take account of the way theologians in the history of the church have thought about the passage, or how other contemporary theologians may hear the text. Instead, the preacher often acts as if she or he is the first person since the text was written to think about the significance of the text for a later community.

This lone-ranger approach to interpretation is alleviated somewhat by the growing number of clergy colleague groups who meet together for sermon preparation (especially around texts assigned by a lectionary). Such groups at least give the preacher the opportunity to hear other perspectives on the text. However, these groups rely mainly on their own imaginations or standard homiletical helps (which seldom contain an explicit theological component), and they seldom engage historical sources or wide-ranging current theological conversation partners.[8] The result is that preachers are often interpretive orphans, deprived of connection with other voices that could add to the theological maturity of the sermon.[9]

BRINGING SYSTEMATIC THEOLOGY INTO BIBLICAL PREACHING: A CONVERSATIONAL MODEL

The preacher can easily bring systematic theology directly into the process of preparing the sermon and into the sermon itself so as to honor the integrity of text, theology, and preacher.

Toward this end, a conversational model of relating scripture, systematic theology, and preaching encourages conscientious, critical engagement.[10]

A key to this approach is to recognize that both the text and systematic theology are each a "Thou," an other.[11] In current philosophical discussion, an other is an entity in its own right. It has its own perspectives, identity, values, and integrity.[12] The other is never only who or what I think it is. It is what it is. As Edward Farley says, "The other, then, is that which I do not and cannot experience in the mode in which I experience myself. It is an 'I' which is not I."[13]

Encountering an other often has significant effects on my world. Perceiving the other as other disrupts my usual patterns of perception and prompts me to pay attention to the otherness of the other. The other interrupts my tendency to see the other as a mirror of my world and me. Being encountered by an other prompts me to identify and assess those points at which my thoughts and actions serve only my own self-interest, and points at which they respect and serve others.

Writing about conversation with others, Mark Kline Taylor, a professor at Princeton Theological Seminary, stresses that such "partners are not really accepted, heard, or included if they are not released from the interlocutor's first impressions and freed from stereotypical and classifying approaches from each other." Taylor is convinced that real interchange among others must bring to the surface differences among all involved.[14] If we bypass the recognition of the other as other, we are likely to focus mainly on what we have in common with the other, and thereby fail to recognize the otherness of the other and see the other as only an extension of ourselves. In that case, we actually violate the integrity of the other. Sometimes the claims of the other can be surprising.[15] David Tracy notices an important function of this encounter: " . . . to attend to the different as other, the different as different, is also to understand the different *as* possible."[16]

When we come face to face with a passage from scripture, we encounter an other who offers us a particular theological interpretation of the world (or a slice of the world). The text voices or assumes an understanding of God, the world, God's purposes in the world, and our response.[17]

The aim of biblical exegesis is to help preacher and congregation recognize the otherness of a biblical passage and hear the distinctive witness of the passage. However, this statement comes with a caveat. Only a generation ago, biblical scholars taught seminary students that, through careful exegesis, they could isolate *the* meaning of a biblical passage. Scholars today, in contrast, remind us that we can never identify the complete meaning of a text. We always perceive a text through a particular mode of interpretation. Different historical, literary, rhetorical, sociological, political, even psychological modes of interpretation prompt us to hear a text in different ways. Furthermore, at different moments in life, interpreters are better able to hear certain things but not others. Our interpretive lenses free us to hear selected aspects of a passage while diminishing our receptivity to others. Not only is the Bible itself pluralistic, so are our interpretations of it. Nevertheless, all methods of contemporary biblical interpretation known to me stress that importance of respecting the otherness of the text.

There are three phases of bringing the Bible and systematic theology into conversation in preaching. I describe these phases as taking place sequentially though in actual practice, their interaction may be much less linear and much more interactive.

Phase One: Naming the Theology of the Text

The preacher needs to help the congregation recognize the otherness of the text and to name the theological claims of the text. The preacher helps the community identify the ways in which the text interprets God, the purposes of God for the world, and our response. Toward this end, it is helpful to review the basic perspectives of the text's theological classification, and then to identify the particularities of the passage. Through exegesis, the preacher invites the congregation to enter the world of the text so as to understand its claims and its otherness.

In this phase, the preacher employs familiar methods of exegesis.[18] She determines the starting and ending points of the text to be sure that the sermon deals with a meaningful unit of scripture. She locates the passage in its sociohistorical context (insofar as this context can be determined with confidence). She identifies the literary genre of the text as well as the characteristics and functions of this genre. She pays attention to sociological, economic, and political perspectives that help us understand the text. She focuses intently on the theological claims of the text.

The preacher seeks to arrive at an understanding of the text that is credible from the standpoints of its historical, literary, and theological contexts. As I mentioned earlier, we can often interpret a text in more than one way. However, the interpretation that the preacher adopts for the sermon needs to be one that is possible from the standpoint of what we know about circumstances in antiquity.

To get a bead on the theological claims of the text, I find it helpful to carry out a conventional exegesis of the text and, in the process, to ask five questions.[19] We can sometimes find answers to these questions in the text itself, but at other times we must draw on wider knowledge of historical, literary, or theological backgrounds. (In this section and the next, I illustrate with the story of God's provision for Elijah and the widow of Zarephath [1 Kgs. 17:8–16].)

1. *To what general theological perspective in the Bible does this text belong—deuteronomist, priestly, apocalyptic, Hellenistic Jewish, other?*

In addition to identifying the theological perspective of the text, it is important to pay attention to points at which the text manifests qualities typical of this classification as well as points at which it differs from the classification. First Kings 17:8–16 belongs to Deuteronomic theology. The Deuteronomists were committed to the notion that obedience to the stipulations of the covenant results in blessing and disobedience results in curse. The Deuteronomic community knew God through study and engaged this passage to learn the path that leads to blessing in order to avoid the path of disobedience that brings the community under curse. The story is contemporized: this narrative is not just a report from the past but is an event in which the contemporary community continues to participate. We are with the Deuteronomic audience that heard the narrative of Elijah and the widow in Zarephath. Their story happens to us.

2. *What exegetical discoveries help clarify the particular claims of this passage (e.g., historical background, assumptions in ancient culture, literary form)?*

First Kings 17:8–16 was given its present form during a historical period when many people embraced Baal and other false deities and abandoned the covenantal call for justice in community. A few people (represented by Elijah) remained faithful, but most of the community ignored or even persecuted them. In 1 Kings 17:1, God intervenes in history to cause a drought in the land as a curse for disobedience. Demonstrating that obedience results in blessing, the text tells us in 17:2–7 that God provides food and water for the prophet at the Wadi Cherith.

The wadi dries up. The water is gone. Although Elijah is faithful, his life appears to be over. However, God does not dry the wadi to curse the prophet. Rather, as the great Deuteronomic teacher, God uses that event to teach the readers the lesson of vv. 8–17.

For sustenance, God sends Elijah to a widow in Zarephath. This move surprises the listeners, for as a widow she is the epitome of the bottom of the social pyramid. She represents the people for whom the Israelites are supposed to maintain covenantal responsibility. Not only that, but she is a Gentile living in Zarephath, a city in Phoenicia. Even more dramatic, she is using the last of her own resources (a handful of meal, a little oil) to prepare the last meal that she and her child will eat before they starve to death. The prophet directs her to prepare a little cake for him, for herself, and for her child. Elijah promises that if she does so, her jar of meal will not empty and her oil will not run out, and, of course, the promise comes true.

The story demonstrates the essence of Deuteronomic theology. Although faced with death, the prophet is faithful to God's command to go to the most unlikely places—here the home of a starving widow in Phoenicia. For her part, the Gentile widow obeys the word of the prophet of the God of Israel. In the process, God blesses the prophet and the widow and her child abundantly. The lesson is clear: the community should remain faithful no matter how profoundly it is threatened, for God will provide for those who are obedient. An irony is not lost on the listener. Though unfaithful people exploit persons at the bottom of the social power structure (such as the widow), God can use these very people as the means to demonstrate the trustworthiness of the Deuteronomic interpretation of God.

3. What are God's purposes for the community in this text?

God's overarching purpose is for the community to renounce idolatry and injustice so it can avoid being cursed, and become faithful so it will be blessed. The specific purpose is to encourage the beleaguered faithful (especially the leaders) of the era in which the Deuteronomists wrote to remain obedient. The text promises that God will provide for them in the midst of threat.

4. What does this text claim regarding the extent and function of divine power in this passage?

What does the community expect God to do? In this theological worldview, God controls nature and history. God speaks directly to Elijah with step-by-step instructions. God sends a drought on the whole community as a curse to teach them the truth of the core of Deuteronomic theology and to prompt them to repentance and faithfulness. God can use any person and circumstance, even those outside the typical circle of the faithful (represented by the widow and Zarephath) for the divine purposes. God can cause the jars of meal and oil to replenish day after day.

5. What response does this text invite?

This text encourages the community to a Deuteronomic style of obedience that includes worship of the living God of Israel and the practice of justice for all in community. It particularly seeks to reinforce those in the community who decide to be faithful even in the face of difficulty.

Phase Two: Bringing the Theology of the Text into Dialogue with Systematic Theology

The next task is to help the congregation bring the theology of the text into conversation with systematic theology, that is, with the core theological convictions of the preacher and the community. The preacher seeks to determine the relationship between the witness of the text and his or her core theology. As Paul Scott Wilson points out, the same text often enters into dialogue with several different doctrines. Wilson wisely suggests that most sermons should focus on dialogue between a text and just one aspect of doctrine or systematic theology to avoid doctrinal or theological overload.[20]

This dimension of the conversation is complicated by the fact that we can understand many texts on two levels—a surface level and a deeper level.[21] At the *surface* level, we hear the text as a straightforward description of God and the world. In this mode, we presume a one-to-one relationship between what the text says and how God and the world operate. These elements are often tied to specific cultural assumptions that we no longer share.

We can also understand texts on a *deeper* level. By this, I mean that we may find in texts values and claims that go beyond the straightforward statement of the text. The text may use culturally conditioned language to speak of experiences and phenomena that occur in our culture but for which we have different language and concepts. Furthermore, we often get important clues for interpreting our worlds from stories that are not factually true. William C. Placher, a noted contemporary theologian, observes,

> After all, we can use different stories to make sense of our lives and use them in different ways. Suppose, for instance, someone grew up reading Horatio Alger and finds in those stories of virtuous hardworking poor boys that reap the rewards of material success after struggle and hardship the key to what life is really about. Such a person would presumably not think of the stories as historically true—one would recognize that they are novels.[22]

Although the story of Horatio Alger is not factual, its view of the world still supplies some people with clues that help them interpret the world. Of course, we must still question the adequacy of such interpretations of the world. The Horatio Alger story, for instance, is not a suitable understanding of the purpose of life for a Christian. But that story illustrates how a surface meaning that is initially unpromising may turn out to be suggestive. The contrast between surface and deeper readings is illustrated below in connection with 1 Kings 17:8–17.

To facilitate the conversation between the theology of the text and that of the preacher, I find it helpful to adapt the questions that are articulated as "Theological Criteria for the Everyday Life of the Church" in chapter 1.[23] (Because they are related to questions 1 through 5, above, I number them 6, 7, and 8.) To illustrate such a conversation, I draw again from 1 Kings 17:8–16, the story of the divine provision for Elijah and the widow of Zarephath, as well as from my own core theological convictions, rooted in relational (process) theology.

6. *Are the theological claims of the text appropriate to the deepest beliefs of the preacher and the community concerning God, the world, God's purposes in the world, and the human response?*

At the surface level, 1 Kings 17:8–16 conflicts with my own theology at three points. First, one of my most tenacious convictions is that God loves the world unconditionally. While God is not pleased with disobedience, a God of unconditional love would not actively inflict drought on a community with its concomitant suffering and death. Second, like many relational theologians, I do not think that God has the power to intervene in history in the straightforward way depicted in this text, that is, by causing drought and filling jars with meal and oil. Third, contrary to the text, leaders and other people in the community of faith who remain obedient in the face of difficulty and opposition often suffer. It is not readily apparent that God always provides for faithful leaders and communities in the way that 1 Kings 17:8–16 claims God provided for Elijah and the widow. I cannot casually commend the theology of this text to a congregation.

At a deeper level, however, significant aspects of this text *are* appropriate to my deepest theological convictions. First, while God does not actively inflict pain on individuals and communities (represented here by drought) because of disobedience, unfaithfulness does set in motion patterns of life that often lead to community collapse. God does not directly punish such communities, but when they fail to cooperate with God's purposes they punish themselves. Second, while God may not have unilateral power to effect dramatic changes in nature and history, God is omnipresent and at work for the good of all. God's power is relational. God works by inviting (luring) people and elements of nature toward blessing. This story affirms that God is present and active for blessing even in the midst of the droughts of the world. While I want to avoid the anachronism of reading the conceptuality of process thought (emphasizing human beings as co-creators with God) into 1 Kings 17:8–16, I notice that both Elijah and the widow cooperated with God and thus facilitated the blessing in Zarephath. Third, I know religious leaders who have been obedient to God's purposes in the face of very difficult circumstances and who report that they have felt divine provision in the midst of their suffering. They feel God's providence through the awareness of the support of others, through prayer and reading the Bible, through partaking at the Table, through the confidence of being aligned with God's purposes. They also feel such providence through similarly unlikely persons and means as the widow of Zarephath. We usually think of Gentile widows (figuratively speaking) as persons for whose welfare the community is responsible. But they sometimes become agents of divine care and community renewal.

7. *Is the witness of the church intelligible? That is, can we understand it? Do the claims of the text cohere with the core of Christian belief and with other things that Christians say and do? Do the claims of the text make sense from the standpoint of the ways in which the community understands the world today?*

The claims of this text are clear. I have no difficulty understanding them. At the deeper level, the text's claims are logically consistent with other things I believe concerning God and the divine purposes for the world. At the surface level, aspects of the text do not make sense according to the way I understand the relationship of God and the world today—for example, God intervening in history to cause the drought and to fill the jars with meal and oil. I cannot invite the prophets and widows of the world to expect meal and oil in their jars. But the deeper reading of the text (see above) eliminates this difficulty.

8. *Are the claims of the text morally plausible, that is, do they call for relationships in the world that are consistent with the preacher's deepest convictions concerning God and God's purposes in the world?*

This text does not sanction human beings mistreating one another or the world of nature. It encourages leaders in the religious community (represented by Elijah) to neither dismiss outsiders and strangers (represented by the widow of Zarephath) nor reduce such persons to objects for whom the community must care. Instead, the text leads us to ask both how God works providentially for such persons and how they might help the community discover God's unconditional love and justice for all. The text implies that God sustains Elijah so that the prophet can continue to call the wider community to obedience and warn it against the results of disobedience.

Phase Three: Incorporating Systematic Theology Directly into the Sermon

The conversation between the theology of the text and that of the preacher usually suggests one of three relationships between systematic theology and the text for the sermon, which congregations often benefit from discussing:[24]

1. The theology of the text may be appropriate to the core theological convictions of the preacher and the congregation. In this case, the preacher needs to help the congregation identify the particular effect of the encounter between the text and the community.

The encounter may reinforce the community's patterns of believing and acting. For instance, a text from the wisdom theology in Proverbs that directs the listener to pay attention to behaviors in nature (as in "Go to the ant, you lazybones, consider its ways, and be wise," Prov. 6:6) supports a preacher and a congregation whose systematic theology stresses experience as a source for interpreting God and the world.

The interaction between the Bible and the congregation may spark the church to recognize possibilities in doctrine, systematic theology, or life and witness that the church has not previously envisioned. For example, a congregation that emphasizes the Holy Spirit as a source of religious ecstasy may encounter a text in the book of Acts that awakens them to an aim of the Spirit in Acts: to bring together persons of diverse racial and ethnic backgrounds in an eschatological community (the church) that embodies the reunion of the human family. The text in Acts helps the community broaden its understanding of the Spirit.

In this mode of relationship, the text may function as a plumb line against which to measure the faithfulness of community life and witness. For instance, an oracle of judgment from the prophet Amos may function as a standard against which the preacher and congregation can measure the ways in which the congregation is just in its own life, as well as in its witness for justice in the larger community.

A text that is appropriate to the church's theology may prompt the church to recall forgotten aspects of its theological core. The postmodern celebration of diversity, for example, can unravel into fragmentation and even animosity among groups, even in the church. Jesus' prayer for the unity of the church in John 17 ("that they may be one") reminds the community to consider its ecumenical theology, which affirms that all Christians share a common life in Jesus Christ—even with congregations with whom we have fundamental disagreements.

Such a text often helps the church experience the divine power that attempts to lure the universe into becoming a cosmic community of love and justice. I am, for instance, writing this chapter at the end of the season of Epiphany, when the story of the transfiguration of Jesus appears in the lectionary. The preacher on Sunday used the transfiguration of Jesus as a lens to help us identify moments in our everyday worlds that are transfigured by the presence of the resurrected Jesus. The sermon itself was an experience of transfiguration.

In addition, the preacher and congregation need to be alert to the possibility that a text or theme in the Bible may call into question an aspect of the church's doctrine or systematic theology. By way of example, Colossians 1:15–20, with its incipient universal vision of salvation, calls into question the theological position of a congregation that advocates an exclusive version of salvation in which only Christians are saved.

2. The theology of the text may partially agree and partially disagree with a community's systematic theology. When this is the case, the sermon must help the community identify points of coherence and points of disagreement. The preacher needs to remain open to the possibility that the theology of the text may call the theology of the contemporary community into question. The Deuteronomic story of God providing for Elijah and the widow of Zarephath (1 Kgs. 17:8–16) is an example of this mode of relationship. The community certainly agrees with the basic claim of the text that divine providence often operates through unlikely means. However, my theological community disagrees with the notion that God can make food appear in an empty jar. We must move from the surface to the deeper level of the text for an intelligible understanding of the latter dimension of the text.

3. The theology of the text and the theology of the preacher may disagree. Indeed, the two theologies can contradict each other. In this case, the sermon must explain the point(s) of disagreement in clear theological terms. For instance, the priestly theologians, seeking to develop a community of holiness, decree, "whoever does any work on [the Sabbath] shall be put to death" (Exod. 35:2). From the perspective of God's unconditional love and unremitting will for justice, this decree is morally implausible.

Theological difficulties of this kind are by no means limited to texts in the First Testament. In fact, the Second Testament can be more brutal than the First. For instance, as the great judgment in the apocalyptic book of Revelation draws to a close, all whose names were not written in the book of life are thrown into a lake of fire where "they will be tormented day and night forever" (20:7–15). The death penalty in Exodus for working on the Sabbath is cruel beyond imagination, but the pain of the victims ends when they lose consciousness. The book of Revelation, in contrast, predicts an eternity of *unrelieved* suffering.

Some cautionary notes must accompany preaching in this mode. The preacher cannot cavalierly dismiss a particular passage but needs to show respect for the text and honor its integrity. Some members of the congregation may be unfamiliar or uncomfortable with the very idea of disagreeing with the Bible. Showing respect for the passage, even while taking issue with aspects of it, will likely avoid alienating them.

Although the teaching of a text may not be fully compatible with the preacher's theology, the *encounter* of theologies of preacher and text may generate effects similar to the ones articulated just above. The encounter might reinforce the community's theology, spark the recognition of previously unnoticed theological insights, function as a plumb line, recall a forgotten text, or reshape a vein of the preacher's theology. As Arthur Van Seters, a Canadian professor of preaching, notices, an encounter with the Bible "has the potential to explode the boundaries of doctrine."[25]

Some preachers may be wary of bringing systematic theology into the sermon, fearing that the congregation will be bored. But theology is boring only if the preacher presents it in a boring way. Chapter 5 includes suggestions for presenting systematic theology in lively homiletical dress. Chapter 7 includes two annotated sermons that illustrate the direct appearance of doctrine and systematic theology in the sermon.

Similarly, pastors in congregations that elevate the Bible as the source of the community's interpretations of God (and disparage other resources) may fear that the congregation will be upset if the preacher gives too much attention to doctrine, especially if the preacher takes exception to the theology of a text. However, my experience (and that of pastors who preach along these lines) is that many people appreciate the broader and more nuanced perspectives provided by theology. They also respond positively to fuller explanations of why preachers and theologians think as they do. When I have criticized the theology of a biblical passage, the reaction has been, "I always wanted to think that way, but I didn't know that I could." In this case, theological criticism becomes an event of liberation. Even when members of the laity are not persuaded, they respect a preacher's clarity and honesty, and they are usually willing to dialogue with the preacher. In any event, the final criterion for whether or not to preach in a certain way is not the congregation's preferences but the preacher's responsibility to speak "the whole counsel of God."

4

The Sermon in the Form of Systematic Theology

I had a difficult time finding an acceptable title for this chapter and for the kind of preaching that it advocates. At one point I called it "Theological Preaching," but, of course, all preaching should be theological in the sense that it interprets life from the perspective of our deepest conviction about God and interprets God from the standpoint of our best insights from life. Even the sermon that originates with the Bible should be theological for we should always refract a biblical witness through a theological lens. Preaching that is not theological has no place in Christian community.

At another point, I considered the title "Preaching the Doctrinal Sermon," for the chapter deals with the idea of beginning the sermon with an element of doctrine instead of a biblical text and offers an exposition of the significance of that doctrinal element. However, in this chapter I commend preaching from a horizon that stretches beyond doctrine as such to include the broader vista of systematic theology.[1]

I settled on "The Sermon in the Form of Systematic Theology" to describe preaching that starts and moves as systematic theology. The title is descriptive though not very elegant. I first explain this kind of preaching.[2] I suggest some considerations to take into account when developing such a sermon and conclude with modes of relationship that may develop between systematic theological affirmations and the congregation. William J.

Carl III, a superb doctrinal preacher, notices that while this perspective may be unusual to pastors who have become accustomed to preaching from the lectionary, it has a long and honorable history in Roman Catholicism and among some Protestants.[3]

WHAT DO WE MEAN BY PREACHING IN THE FORM OF SYSTEMATIC THEOLOGY?

An easy way to get a handle on the sermon that starts and moves as systematic theology is to contrast it with expository preaching. In the latter, the preacher begins the preparation of the sermon with the exposition of a passage or theme from the Bible and asks, "How does our encounter with this part of the Bible enhance our understanding of God and Christian life and witness?" The expository sermon is controlled by the need to understand the text and to work out a theologically satisfactory relationship between the text and the congregation.[4]

In contrast, the sermon that begins and moves as systematic theology centers not in the exposition of a biblical passage but in an element of doctrine or systematic theology. The preacher begins the preparation of the sermon by identifying a discrete affirmation from doctrine or systematic theology and develops the sermon around that theological assertion. *The theological affirmation functions in the sermon much like the biblical text or theme functions in an expository sermon.* The preacher asks, "How does our encounter with this theological statement enhance our understanding of God and Christian life and witness?" The sermon that starts and moves as systematic theology aims (1) to help the congregation understand a particular theological affirmation and (2) to work out a satisfactory relationship between the theological assertion and the congregation.

Sermons of this kind, for example, could focus on an article in an affirmation of faith or other doctrinal statement. A pastor might develop a sermon on part of an article in the Apostolic affirmation of faith in which the congregation confesses, "I believe . . . in the communion of saints." The sermon would explain how the church in history and its contemporary setting understands the notion "communion of saints." The preacher would answer the question, "How is this idea important for the life of the congregation?" While the message might incorporate materials from the Bible that inform this theme, the preacher's overriding responsibility is to offer a comprehensive theological interpretation of the communion of saints for today's congregation.

This type of sermon could also originate from a perspective found in a formal work of systematic theology. For example, Marjorie Suchocki, who teaches at Claremont School of Theology, offers an understanding of original sin that could be the subject of a sermon that starts and moves as systematic theology.

> The traditional Christian understanding of sin has had a dual focus, the one personal and the other impersonal. Sin as personal indicates a violation of relationships, resulting in a state of alienation from God, nature, one another, and the self. The condition of alienation, however, is one into which we have been born. If there is a sense in which sin precedes us, then obviously there is an impersonal element in sin. This has been described as original sin and the demonic. Frequently Christians have personalized these powers and projected them away from us as a nonhuman being, a devil, whose temptation of humanity in its very beginnings resulted in transgression and original sin. Process theology suggests a more tragic view, naming the cumulative acts of human beings in society as the source of the demonic. We are ourselves corporately responsible for the societies we create and the ill effects they engender. The demonic element is that we are each individually born into a society we did not create; insofar as it contains powers of destruction, these originate prior to our being. These powers can and do overwhelm us, involving us in the condition of alienation that is manifested in personal sin. In the grip of these powers, we continue to perpetuate them. Thus in a process world, the past can be understood as the conveyor of original sin and the demonic.[5]

The sermon could describe this phenomenology of sin and probe ways in which the encounter with this theological statement helps interpret the congregation's experience.

This kind of interpretation can be of immense pastoral value in helping both individuals and groups understand broken and painful circumstances in which they find themselves but that they did not create. This phenomenology explains to African Americans, for example, why they suffer under racism when they have done nothing to bring it on themselves. It can also help people recognize their own complicity in perpetuating original sin by, for example, explaining to European Americans how they are complicit in continuing racism.

Beyond naming the effect of original sin and the demonic, however, Christian preaching is seldom content to name sin. The preacher is called to announce the good news of God's renewing presence, and consequently, would likely also help the individual and the congregation discern God's efforts to transform situations of original sin into situations of blessing. The minister also wants to help the congregation recognize the degree of freedom that individuals and groups have (no matter how slight) to shape the present and the future differently from the past and so as to optimize relationships. For instance, the minister can note, while African Americans (individually and in community) cannot undo racism *en toto*, they can sometimes act with a freedom and creativity that defies racism. European Americans, likewise, can take steps in partnership with African Americans to create a future free of the relational distortions of racism.

The theological sources for sermons are numerous:[6]

> Historic ecumenical affirmations, such as Apostles' Affirmation of Faith, Nicene Affirmation of Faith, Chalcedonian formulation.

> Historic denominational affirmations of faith, such as the *Book of Confessions* of the Presbyterian Church (U.S.A.), which contains items such as the Heidelberg Catechism, the Westminster Confession of Faith, and the Shorter and Larger Catechisms; the *Book of Concord* of Lutheranism (containing items such as the Augsburg Confession, the Small Catechism, the Large Catechism, the Formula of Concord); the Creed of the Council of Trent; the Thirty-Nine Articles (Episcopal and Anglican churches); the Twenty-Five Articles

of Religion (accepted by the African Methodist Episcopal Church, the African American Methodist Episcopal Church Zion, the Christian Methodist Episcopal Church, and the United Methodist Church); the General Rules of the same churches; the Baptist Faith and Message and the various other confessions around which Baptists gather.

Contemporary affirmations of faith, such as the Theological Declaration of Barmen, the Confession of 1967 of the Presbyterian Church (U.S.A.), the United Church of Christ Statement of Faith, the Statement of Faith of the United Church of Canada, the Preamble to the Design of the Christian Church (Disciples of Christ), the United Methodist Statement of "Our Theological Task," the World Methodist Social Affirmation.

Documents that officially or unofficially represent theological viewpoints of the church on particular issues. Many churches adopt resolutions or make other declarations that sum up their thinking on a particular topic at a particular time, for example, the *Book of Resolutions* of the United Methodist Church, which is prepared after each General Conference and covers matters ranging from the theology of the natural world through matters of human community, including social life, economics, and the political world. Similar resolutions are published after the General Assemblies of the Presbyterian Church (U.S.A.), the Christian Church (Disciples of Christ), the United Church of Christ, and other bodies.

Occasional writings of historic or contemporary figures of the church that function (sometimes informally) to summarize aspects of the church's beliefs, for example, various papal encyclicals, works of Augustine, Martin Luther, John Calvin, Menno Simons, John Wesley, Thomas Cranmer, Alexander Campbell, Barton Stone.

Writings of systematic theologians that interpret the above materials and that help the Christian community theologically interpret the world. See the list of representative systematic theologians in chapter 1 (p. 10).

Some preachers may object to this, arguing that documents that officially or unofficially represent viewpoints of the church, not to mention the writings of historic figures of the church and contemporary systematic theologians, do not have the same theological standing in the church as historic or contemporary affirmations of faith and, therefore, should not be a focal point for preaching. It is true that contemporary interpretations do not have the status of doctrine, but they are often influential in shaping the beliefs and practices of a congregation or a preacher. A congregation will frequently benefit from naming these sources and their effects, and coming to a critical interpretation of the role these writings actually play in what it believes and does.

For instance, although John Wesley's *Standard Sermons* do not have formal theological force in world Wesleyan communities, they provide considerable guidance for Wesleyan belief and witness. Material from the *Standard Sermons* could easily become the starting point for a sermon that explains why the viewpoint in the sermon came to expression, how it has guided the church, and how the church might relate to it today.

DEVELOPING A SERMON
IN THE FORM OF SYSTEMATIC THEOLOGY

The preparation of a sermon that starts and moves as systematic theology includes moments of research and reflection that parallel those that are a part of the development of a sermon that originates from the Bible.

The preparation of this sermon begins with the pastor selecting an element of doctrine or theology to focus on and honoring its otherness. Respect for the otherness of an element of doctrine or systematic theology (see chapter 3, in regard to biblical texts) is foundational. An other is an entity with its own integrity, identity, and perspectives. When we come face to face with an element of doctrine or systematic theology, we encounter an other who offers us a particular theological interpretation of the world. Ministers can commit a form of eisegesis of a doctrine or a segment of theology by disregarding the otherness of the doctrine or systematic theology, and by reading their own perspectives into the material.

When preparing to preach from a historic or contemporary affirmation of faith, we might carry out an exegesis of that affirmation that is similar to the exegesis of a biblical text.[7] The following are among the key steps in such an exegesis:

Reconstruct the historical context that led to the theological statement that is the subject of the sermon. What was happening in the wider culture and in the church? Take account of social, political, economic, and religious factors that played into the formulation of the affirmation.

Locate the meanings of words and ideas as understood in the historical period in which the document was written.

Show how texts or themes from the Bible relate to the affirmation of faith, the doctrine, or the vector in systematic theology that is the pivotal point of the sermon. A sermon can often show continuity between the affirmation and certain biblical materials. A congregation's awareness of the pluralism of the Bible and Christian tradition and theology can be enhanced when the preacher calls attention to incongruities between the Bible and the theological orientation of the preacher.

Reflect on how the central theological point of the doctrine relates to other doctrines and to other aspects of the congregation's life and witness.

Be clear about the specific theological claim at the center of doctrine and how that claim is interpreted in the preacher's contemporary systematic theology.

Name the effects of perspective of the doctrine or theological statement for the contemporary congregation.

Consider what the sermon needs to do in order to help the claim come alive in an optimum way for the congregation.

As I note in chapter 5, the preacher can often bring material from historical theology directly into the sermon. This has the benefit of helping the congregation more vividly picture and accurately feel the circumstances that gave rise to the theological claims. Including such material in the sermon helps the congregation grasp the importance of the doctrine or theological idea and heightens its interest.

Much of the time the preacher can move directly from the setting and claim of the text to the present situation. At times, especially when dealing with historical texts, however, the preacher may make an analogy between the situation in which the doctrine or theological claim came to expression and our situation in much the same the same way that a preacher makes an analogy between the situation of a biblical text and our world.[8]

The doctrine of the Trinity is an example of how illuminating it can be for a preacher and a congregation to understand a doctrine or a systematic theology from the perspective of the historical circumstances that influenced it. Clark M. Williamson has noted that although church historians sometimes say that Arius sparked Christian thinking about the Trinity in the fourth century, both Marcion and the Gnostics had much earlier influenced Christian thinking on the doctrine of the Trinity. Marcion taught the anti-Jewish theme that the creator and redeemer were two distinct entities and that the redeemer (Jesus Christ) was superior to the creator (the God of the First Testament) so that Christ replaced the vengeful God of the Jewish people. The Gnostics believed that the human being was composed of two parts—the soul that is the essential nonmaterial part of the self, and the body that is the nonessential material part of the self. They argued that the God of the Jewish people had trapped the soul in the body and that Christ had to save us by liberating the nonmaterial soul from the material body.

Whereas both Marcion and the Gnostics taught that Christianity superseded Judaism, other branches of the church, in reflecting on the Trinity, made just the opposite point, as Williamson shows:

> The question, "Who is God?" or "Which God is incarnate in Jesus Christ?" is answered [by the early church] by saying: The God who created the world, liberated Israel from captivity in Egypt, was with Israel in the wilderness, in the

entrance to the land of Canaan, who "dwelt" with Israel in the ark of the covenant, in the temple, who went with Israel into exile, the God whose "dwelling" (the root meaning of *Shekinah* = presence) is with us even in the valley of the shadow of death, the God who became flesh in Jesus Christ and "dwelt among us, full of grace and truth," this "Emmanuel" (God with us) and this God who eschatologically will ultimately redeem God's good creation—this is the One of whom we speak when we name/identify God as "Trinity."[9]

One foundational purpose of the doctrine of the Trinity, then, is to assert for Christians a positive connection between Judaism and Christianity.

This reading of the emergence of the notion of the Trinity is particularly important for Williamson's own post-Holocaust systematic theology, *Way of Blessing, Way of Life*, in which he critiques anti-Jewish elements in Christian theology and recovers continuities between Judaism and Christianity. Awareness of this context illumines Williamson's summary statement regarding the church's teaching of the Trinity.

> The doctrine of the Trinity is the church's way of asserting that the God it worships is the God of Israel and of the Israel of God. The Trinity names or identifies the God who is incarnate in Jesus Christ and active in the Holy Spirit as the God of Israel and of the scriptures. It is a way of summarizing/ describing the activity of God in the history of salvation, God as related to the world and history.[10]

Far from showing the superiority of Christianity to Judaism, this interpretation of the doctrine of the Trinity suggests a sermon that calls attention to an indissoluble commonality between these two religious movements that makes anti-Judaism completely unacceptable in the Christian house.

When discussing the theological interpretation of the Bible in chapter 3, I discussed the motifs of surface and deeper witnesses that we may draw from a text. The surface witness is the straightforward meaning of a passage or idea in the language and presuppositions of the culture in which the text came to life. We may today find it difficult to believe or endorse aspects of the surface hearing. However, we can often identify a deeper meaning, that is, aspects of the passage or idea may have dimensions that transcend its particular cultural formulation. Ancient and contemporary communities may share a common experience that is expressed in different cultural forms.

This distinction is sometimes helpful when working with doctrines articulated in times and cultures that are quite different from those of the congregation. For instance, when reciting the Nicene Affirmation of Faith, the congregation says, "We believe in one Lord, Jesus Christ . . . For us and our salvation, he came down from heaven, was incarnate of the Holy Spirit and the Virgin Mary, and became truly human." The language of coming down from heaven and being born of a virgin presupposes a cosmos with a heavenly world located spatially above the earthly one.

At the surface level, many people today find it difficult to think that Jesus literally came down from a heavenly realm to this one, and/or to think that Jesus was conceived (or born) from a virgin. These elements of the affirmation of faith are mythological ways of accounting for the incarnation. The deeper witness is that through Jesus Christ, we experience God with us. When developing a sermon on this part of the Nicene Affirmation, the preacher would explain not only the circumstances in the history of the church that made the incarnation a pivotal notion, but also both the surface and deeper dimensions of the meaning of the text. Using such conceptuality, the preacher can help the congregation members understand how they can robustly recite this part of the affirmation of faith.

Historic and contemporary affirmations did not drop from the sky in a pure form. They resulted from discussion and debate about how best to interpret Christian faith in a particular moment of history. Such interchange continues as Christian communities try to sort through what they most deeply believe. One of the responsibilities of preaching in connection with systematic theology is to help the congregation identify its core theological convictions by entering into conversation with elements of the tradition and contemporary theological voices. In this respect, the sermon is less like a photocopier that simply reproduces material from the past (or from other places in the present) and hands it to the congregation and more like a union meeting in which members of the community wrestle together to determine fruitful paths to working with management and customers.

The church must on occasion criticize and even reject affirmations from the past or present that do not measure up to the best of its contemporary theological interpretation. At the same time, today's church needs to attend to the possibility that encounters with theological worlds of the past can help us recognize points at which contemporary theological thinking is deficient.

MODES OF RELATIONSHIP BETWEEN SYSTEMATIC THEOLOGY AND THE CONGREGATION

The sermon that starts and moves as systematic theology is usually in one of six relationships with the congregation (see below). The relationship depends on how the theological claim of the sermon intersects with the theological location of the congregation. This relationship may be plotted on a spectrum that runs from congruence between the theology of the sermon and that of the congregation to fundamental divergence.

The relationship between the theology of the sermon and the theology and witness of the congregation often suggests directions for the sermon. When the theology of the sermon and the theology of the community converge, the preacher needs mainly to clarify, enlarge, reinforce, remind, and motivate. When the theologies of the message and the listeners diverge, the preacher must help the congregation recognize the points of difference and encourage the community members to bring their actual beliefs and actions into line with what they should believe and do. The relationship between the theology of the sermon and that of the congregation can take one of six modes.

1. The sermon in the form of systematic theology may *reinforce or clarify* the community's actual beliefs and attitudes. For

instance, Luther's doctrine of justification by grace through faith is the fulcrum of Lutheranism. In a sermon on this doctrine, the preacher would define justification as right relationship with God. He or she might indicate that early in his life, Luther thought that a human being could be justified only by performing satisfactory works, yet was painfully aware of his inability to create a right relationship with God based on merit. Reading Romans awakened in the young Luther the realization that justification takes place as a result of God's grace by faith. The preacher would define grace and faith.

Lutheran preachers need periodically to explain and reinforce the concept of justification by grace through faith because it is central to Lutheran identity and because so much in contemporary culture is based on achievement or works. Our world rewards people for their successful efforts (and punishes people for their lack of success) in school, on the job, in athletics, in volunteerism. Preaching this doctrine reinforces the centrality of justification by grace in a world in which people are constantly taught to justify themselves by works in other arenas of life. In this respect, justification by grace is countercultural. Along the way, the preacher would want to warn Lutherans against turning this doctrine on its head by thinking of faith as a work that believers must perform in order to merit God's grace.

2. The sermon that starts and moves as systematic theology may spark the Christian community to *enlarge its theological vision or to recognize fresh possibilities* in its theology, life, and witness. For example, authority in the church has largely centered in the Bible and in Christian tradition as formulated and interpreted by males. Feminist theology calls attention to the experience of women as a resource and norm for theological reflection.[11] Feminist theologians typically believe that women's experiences of love, nurturing, strength in the face of struggle, and mutuality signal aspects of God's purposes for all and find that experiences of limitation, domination, and abuse deny God's purposes.

Preachers aligned with feminist theology will help the church enlarge its theological vision by recovering feminine images of the divine in the Bible and Christian tradition, as well as aspects of women's history and leadership that have been forgotten, unnoticed, rewritten, or suppressed (typically by males). Such pastors will help the church recognize emancipatory impulses in Christian tradition. In addition, preachers touched by feminism can help the church recognize that the experience of women can be a locus of authority in the church.[12] Indeed, many feminists conclude that biblical texts or theological themes that justify the oppression of any person are not authoritative. Whereas much Christian history presumes a pyramidal model of relationships between women and men (with men superior to women in the home and in the church), feminists help the Christian community envision egalitarian relationships for women and men in the home and wider world.

3. The sermon in the form of systematic theology can serve an especially important pastoral function by *helping a community sort through theological matters about which the community is uncertain or conflicted*. The current ecclesial discussion regarding homosexuality is a case in point. The church is sharply divided over the issue of whether a person with a homosexual orientation can (a) be a Christian and (b) serve in positions of leadership in the church. The Bible does not provide a definitive answer because it discusses homosexuality directly in only five (or six) very brief texts. While all of these passages look askance at homosexuality, none of them presumes the same understanding of homosexuality that many people advocate today, namely that homosexuality is a God-given life orientation. Christian tradition, likewise, contains little sustained discussion of homosexuality, though we can now recognize occasional homosexual voices from the historic Christian community.

The Bible and Christian tradition cannot settle the issue by themselves. A systematic theological perspective is needed. Systematic theology considers homosexuality from the standpoint of a coherent theological exploration of human sexuality that takes into account the experience of persons with same-gender orientations who enter into long-term covenantal relationships. This exploration also considers data from psychology and sociology, as well as from the physical sciences.

The theologian-preacher asks, "What does God intend in the sexual relationship? Can homosexual relationships manifest this intention?"

4. A sermon that starts and moves as systematic theology may help a congregation *remember aspects of theology that the community has forgotten (or learn aspects that the community never knew).* For example, my denomination, the Christian Church (Disciples of Christ), partakes of the breaking of the loaf every Sunday. Despite this frequency, many members are not well informed about how our church understands the theological significance of the meal. Indeed, many Disciples think of the sacred meal as little more than a time to sit quietly and meditate. Theological instruction is needed in order to deepen the congregation's experience at the Table.

The theology of my denomination shares the Reformed understanding of the Supper as an outward symbol of an inward spiritual grace that assures us of God's faithfulness to us (and to all). This theological formulation is not articulated just that way in any single biblical passage. The Reformed understanding of the Supper is informed by meal traditions in the First and Second Testaments and in other Jewish literature, by the various accounts of the Last Supper in the Gospels, and by other teachings in the Second Testament. But the Reformed notion is fuller and more explicit and is stated with more eloquence than the content of any one passage in the Bible.

When preaching with an eye toward doctrine, the preacher would aim to help the congregation understand and appreciate the larger theological perspective. The sermon would seek to help the congregation grasp the practical significance of this theological understanding for their own lives. The preacher might ask, "What are some circumstances in the congregation when this understanding of the sacred meal is of direct help to the congregation?" A homily on the subject would also help the congregation understand how this notion of the breaking of the loaf is related to other aspects of theology. It could go like this: The breaking of the bread and the pouring of the cup represent the unconditional love of God for all. The church likewise is to witness to God's love for all. The practice of "open communion," that is, inviting all to partake of the loaf and the cup, is a norm by which to measure the inclusiveness of the Christian community in all other aspects of its life and witness.

5. A sermon that starts and moves as systematic theology can help the community reinterpret elements of Christian tradition in such a way as to *overcome difficulties in the tradition and to help the congregation discover revitalized theological promise*. In company with feminists, womanists, and mujeristas, professor of preaching L. Susan Bond, author of *Trouble with Jesus*, identifies "christological blunders" in the various ways that the church has formulated its understandings of Jesus Christ. These blunders include separation of the cross and the resurrection, uncritical triumphalism, spirit/body dualism, the compromise between justice and evil, confusion regarding the relationship of the two natures of Christ, the compromise between power and love, individualism, and approval of suffering and picturing God as an abusive parent.[13] Many of these blunders contribute to the diminution and abuse of women, and have distorted Christian community and witness.

Bond takes the Chalcedonian formulation metaphorically so as to reinterpret its Christology to overcome these blunders. She describes her project as a salvage operation in which workers save everything they can and discard what's damaged.[14]

Chalcedon holds that Jesus Christ is composed of two natures—human and divine—that are "unmixed, unchanged, undivided, and inseparable."[15] This metaphorical approach brackets questions of ontology, that is, what we can say literally about the intermingling of the divine and human in Jesus Christ. Instead, Bond notices that the stories of the actions and teachings of Jesus Christ function symbolically in the Christian community as "a disclosure of God's orientation and activities towards the world." In this way, "we can reclaim the *religious meaning* (if not the metaphysical meaning) of the Chalcedonian claim that Jesus was both human and divine. We do not have to accept the metaphysical physics of the creed in terms of literal substance and person."[16]

From this symbolic perspective, the symbol "Jesus Christ" represents or makes God present to us. What the narratives of

Jesus depict him saying and doing reveal God "salvaging the world," that is, remaking the world into a community of love, mutual support, abundance for all, and joy. "Jesus reveals divine aims through ordinary human activities." Consequently, the church comes to understand not only that "ordinary human activities can reveal divine purposes," but that "*we* reveal God when we do ordinary things for [God's] purposes: when we lobby for welfare reform, when we forgive the wrongs that others have done to us, when we share a common meal with folks like us."[17]

6. The sermon in the form of systematic theology can *call into question and even correct what the community believes*. In demonstration, I will amplify my discussion of Luther's doctrine of justification by grace through faith, begun above. Luther thought that the Jewish people of the first century advocated justification by works. Obedience to the law was the justifying work par excellence. The reformer saw Judaism as a religion of legalism concerned only with empty, external actions and ceremonies. According to Luther, Jesus Christ revealed the falsehood of the Jewish perception of justification by works and, in consequence, the superiority of Christianity over Judaism. Luther's polemics against Judaism joined other impulses in historical theology in drifting into anti-Semitism that helped form the bias against the Jewish people in central Europe and eventuated in the Holocaust. The preacher needs to help the congregation draw a bead on Luther's thinking and its pernicious effects.

Contemporary theology recognizes that Luther misperceived the Jewish understanding of grace, works, and law. We now know that the Jewish community in the first century also believed in a God who had brought them into right relationship with the divine through grace revealed in the Exodus (and many other events) and inscribed in covenant and Torah in the same way that the event of Jesus Christ reveals God's grace for the church and its gentile constituency. Whereas the church formerly stressed the difference and discontinuity between Judaism and Christianity, more recent investigations point to similarity and continuity. Indeed, the preacher can help the congregation see that Christians are able to understand Jesus

Christ as a manifestation of God's grace because of the great template of grace that is revealed in Judaism.

This theological corrective does not invalidate Luther's point that we are justified by grace through faith. That doctrine stands by itself and does not require a discredited portrait of Judaism. Indeed, the pastor can preach justification by grace as something shared by Christian and Jewish communities. Whereas Christians know the gracious God through Jesus Christ, Jewish people know the gracious God through covenant and Torah.

Many congregations welcome preaching that starts and moves as systematic theology. For instance, congregations want to know not simply what the book of Revelation teaches regarding the last thing, but what contemporary people can believe concerning these things. Listeners appreciate knowing what their pastor and denomination believe. Even when a congregation's beliefs do not square with those of its pastor or denomination, the interchange can be thought provoking.

5

Making Theology
Lively in the Sermon

Earlier I reported telling a friend that I was working on a book on preaching systematic theology. My friend replied, "That sounds dull." While I find it hard to imagine how anyone could find systematic theology dull, I admit that occasional works of systematic theology can be hard to follow. They sometimes use words that are unfamiliar and hard to understand or keep the discussion at an abstract level.

In this chapter I consider some practical things that a preacher can do to help make theology lively in the sermon. They include creating or selecting a form or movement for the sermon, beginning the sermon in a way that suggests that the topic is of interest and importance, clearly defining the topic, giving the theological theme a face by sketching a salient point from its history, calling attention to denominational perspectives, telling stories that show how theology comes to life, showing connections between theology and the everyday world, naming one's own convictions forthrightly, dealing seriously with questions, and embodying the sermon in a tone appropriate to its theological direction.

Preachers should use concrete, vivid, and evocative language in the sermon. Such language that is closely related to life helps the congregation enter the world of systematic theology.

CREATING OR SELECTING
A MOVEMENT FOR THE SERMON

There is no single form or structure for doctrinal or theological preaching. The preacher needs to create or select a movement for the sermon that promises to give the congregation a good opportunity to listen attentively. When bringing systematic theology prominently into the sermon, I am attracted to preaching (and hearing) deductive, linear sermons that state ideas clearly. Deduction is easy to follow. However, inductive approaches can be valuable, especially when the congregation resists theological reflection or thinks that a subject is boring. *Patterns for Preaching: A Sermon Sampler* collects thirty-four approaches to sermons.[1] My students typically respond, "I never imagined so many kinds of preaching!" Yet, thirty-four is only a small sample. There are as many ways of preaching as there are preachers.

Some traditional forms of expository preaching have built-in places for systematic theology. The Puritan Plain Style, for instance, contains three central parts: exegesis of the text, theological reflection, and application to the world of the congregation. Many traditional forms of expository preaching can be adapted to sermons that start and move as systematic theology. For example, Paul Scott Wilson's popular *Four Pages of the Sermon* can be adjusted as follows:[2] page 1 sketches the trouble in the world that gave rise to the doctrine; page 2 shows how our world is similarly troubled; page 3 develops how the doctrine addressed the trouble in its world; page 4 shows how the doctrine brings good news to troubled situations.

Some conventional forms of topical preaching lend themselves to the sermon that starts and moves as systematic theology. For example, when using a model based on practical theological reasoning, the sermon begins by describing and listening to the experience that gave rise to an element of doctrine, engages in critical theological reflection on the doctrine, and helps the congregation make a decision to accept (or reject) the doctrine and envision how to live from the perspective of its decision.[3]

My impression is that most preachers develop sermons in the same way that an author writes a novel.[4] The preacher engages in background study, and then begins to prepare the sermon proper without knowing completely how the sermon will unfold. The preacher has a sense of direction, but the sermon often takes on a life of its own.

The important thing is that the preacher reflect critically on the movement of the sermon in relationship to the content of the message and the situation of the congregation. When a congregation is initially resistant to the claim of the sermon, the preacher may be well advised to select an inductive approach that allows the congregation to ease into the sermon. In an environment of resistance, a deductive pattern that announces the major claim at the beginning of the sermon may turn off people before they even have a chance to consider the claim.

BEGIN THE SERMON IN A WAY THAT ENGAGES INTEREST AND SUGGESTS IMPORTANCE

The preacher can often whet the appetite of the congregation for systematic theology by beginning the sermon in a way that reveals the direction of the sermon while suggesting that the theological content to be explored is interesting and important. In a deductive sermon, the preacher might disclose the sermon's theological claim at the outset. In an inductive sermon, the preacher might suggest the direction of the sermon without giving away the major claim.

René Rodgers Jensen, co-minister of a congregation in Omaha, Nebraska, begins a sermon on a theological understanding of salvation by drawing on an experience from her youth. The sermon is one in a series that she mentions.

> I grew up in a little town in southeast Texas. We had one movie theater. No bowling alley. No Pizza Hut, though we did have the Dixie Queen, where most of the high school kids hung out. No mall, of course, or even any

stores that stayed open past 7:00 P.M., except for the 7-11. In those pre-cable TV days, no one got more than three channels on their televisions, and then only if you had a really good antenna.

Needless to say, we said yes to nearly anything to do. So, when an acquaintance invited my best friend Gail and me to Teen Night at the annual summer revival, we went. Neither Gail nor I attended the church where the revival was held. I was a member of a struggling little Disciples congregation and my friend Gayle attended an equally small though slightly more prosperous Episcopal Church. Needless to say my church and Gail's church did not have summer revivals.

I have only one clear memory of the revival. It happened near the end of the evening. Our acquaintance, inspired by the events of the evening, grabbed Gail by the arm and asked if Gail had been saved. Now this is not language that you hear very often in an Episcopal church, and Gail was both puzzled by the question and surprised by the very un-Episcopalian ardor with which it had been asked, not to mention that she was in some pain from the grip our acquaintance had on Gail's arm. "Saved?" Gail burst out. "Saved from what?"

It was, I thought then and think now, a very good question. We talk about salvation, and say that Jesus is our savior, but seldom do a very good job of saying just what salvation means in our church. What are we saved from? What are we saved for? So it seems a good idea, in this Summer Sermon Series about the fundamentals of God and the Christian faith, to spend a few minutes asking, "What do we mean when we say we are saved?"[5]

With a touch of humor that nonetheless shows respect for the church in which the revival was held, the preacher uses this incident to focus the conversation that will ensue in the sermon but does not give away how the sermon will define salvation. The sermon then explores understandings of salvation in the Bible, in church history, in the denomination with which the congregation is in covenant, and in the theological perspective of the preacher.

CLEARLY DEFINE THE THEOLOGICAL TOPIC

Paul Scott Wilson points out that the sermon needs to define clearly the theological topic that is its focus.[6] Typically, the preacher needs to define even basic theological terms, and always in an engaging way.

Barbara Brown Taylor, one of the most evocative preachers of the early twenty-first century, speaks of four steps Christian tradition has often prescribed for people seeking renewed life: confession, pardon, penance, and restoration. She lyrically defines each term and its significance. We confess our sin, and receive pardon (forgiveness). Many North American Christians go no further. Taylor, however, defines and calls attention to the importance of penance—the act of making restitution for ways that we have violated community with God and one another.

> While penance has all but disappeared from our vocabulary, it was once the church's best tool for getting over [the hump of receiving forgiveness but then not doing anything to restore community]. Once a person had confessed her sins and received assurance of pardon, she voluntarily took on specific acts of penance, which were baby steps in the direction of new life. If she had stolen vegetables from a neighbor's garden, she might volunteer to weed the garden every other day for a month. If she had slandered someone, she might visit all the households where she had done that and set the record straight.[7]

Taylor stresses that penance is "not punishment" but "repair." She helps listeners recognize the importance of going beyond the words and good feelings of pardons to the actual restoration of relationships in community. In its traditional sense, penance does not earn pardon (in which case it would be a work) but follows pardon.[8]

With respect to theological terms, a minister can take nothing for granted. The sermon should define even basic terms (such as Holy Spirit, sin, faith, righteousness) so that preacher and congregation communicate on the same channel.

GIVE THE THEOLOGICAL THEME A FACE

The preacher can often help a doctrine or an aspect of systematic theology come alive by giving it a human face, that is, by telling something of the people, events, and struggles that brought that element of doctrine or theology to expression. This kind of material in the sermon helps listeners recognize that doctrine and theology have a direct relationship with every life and are not abstract and distant. Such material also alerts the community to the historical conditioning (and hence relativity) of doctrine and theology. This approach may also prompt today's congregation to be as creative in thinking about fundamental theological matters today as earlier generations.

For example, one of the most famous theological statements in the last half of the twentieth century was Paul Tillich's admonition, "Simply accept the fact that you are accepted."[9] While this theme is compelling when heard by itself, it is even more so when a congregation understands Tillich's perception of the existential situation in mid-century North America and the intersection of Tillich's life with that situation. According to Tillich, each era of history is dominated by particular existential concerns. In each era, the church correlates its understanding of the gospel and theology so as to address the concerns of that era.[10]

Tillich had grown up in Germany. After living through the devastation of the First World War, his subsequent hopes for a utopian community did not materialize. He was a university professor when the Nazis came to power, but was dismissed from his post when he took a stand against the Nazi party. After considerable struggle, he left Germany to teach at Union Theological Seminary in New York. With Tillich's biography in mind, we can hear aspects of his own life struggle when he speaks of the main issues of his own time: "It is not an exaggeration to say that today [human beings experience their] present situation in terms of disruption, conflict, self-destruction, meaninglessness, and despair in all realms of life." Consequently, Tillich understood the central issue of his time as "the question of a reality in which the self-estrangement of our existence is overcome, a reality of reconciliation and reunion, of creativity, meaning, and hope."[11]

When Tillich's theology has a human face illumined by his own life and times, we hear his meditation on acceptance not simply as a psychological condition, but as an analogue of grace with great existential power. In the midst of a world of disruption, estrangement, and meaninglessness, we hear a voice saying, "You are accepted. *You are accepted.* Accepted by that which is greater than you, and the name of which you do not know. *Simply accept the fact that you are accepted!*"[12] When that takes place "we experience grace." When we accept the fact that we are accepted by the One who is greater than we, we experience grace that enables us not only to make our way through the disruptions of life but also to envision life in its whole, to experience reconciliation and reunion with others, and to find meaning.[13]

CALL ATTENTION TO DENOMINATIONAL PERSPECTIVE

A local Christian community often benefits from learning the perspective of the denomination or theological movement of which the community is a part. This perspective helps the community understand the movement's perspective on an aspect of doctrine or systematic theology. Information about a church's beliefs can be illuminating and even empowering. I recollect a person who, upon hearing such a perspective, burst out with amazement, "I never knew we were supposed to believe that!"

Marjorie Suchocki, a United Methodist who teaches at Claremont School of Theology, shows how elegantly a voice from the Wesleyan tradition can add to a sermon on the theological claim that God is continuously creating, even today.

> But *how* is God creating now, as then? A very practical way to approach it may be to turn to some interesting words that John Wesley preached in that little book that I often quote,

> *A Plain Account of Christian Perfection.* Smack in the middle of
> the book on page 69, Wesley speaks about the creation of
> Adam. Adam was "required . . . to use, to the glory of God,
> all the powers with which he was created. Now he was cre-
> ated free from any defect, either in his understanding or his
> affections. His body was then no clog to the mind." What
> kind of a creation is this? Just as the psalmist bespeaks a
> responsive creation, singing out the praise of its maker, even
> so Wesley speaks of a responsive Adam. But the Wesleyan
> take on Adam's responsiveness is particularly instructive.
> God, in creating Adam, required Adam to use that which had
> been given to him. And this applied not simply to one aspect
> of himself, such as his mind. Rather, Adam was to use *all* the
> powers with which he was created to the glory of God. Mind,
> affections, body—all were to be developed to the fullest, and
> in this development, God the creator would be glorified.
>
> The implication, surely, is that God creates a creature full
> of potentiality, and that God calls the creation itself to
> develop that potentiality.[14]

Suchocki then helps us recognize how God is "brooding over
us," and calling us to participate with God in fashioning our
powers of intellect, affection, and body. God is at work as creator through our "restlessness . . . to think more deeply,"
through "the yearning to open yourself more fully to love,"
through seeking for an "optimum" of possibilities for one's
physical condition.[15]

By recommending that a preacher bring forward the denomination's teaching on an issue, I do not intend to encourage
denominational tribalism. But particular churches do have particular emphases. People often join a particular church because
they have identified intuitively with aspects of that church's
perspective. Bringing the denomination's beliefs to the surface
of the sermon helps such people identify and more fully appreciate those intuitive associations. Of course, the reverse is also
true. Individuals and congregations may disagree with aspects
of the denomination's historic teaching. In this case, verbaliz-
ing the movement's theological position allows the congregation to enter into critical reflection with what the denomination
actually commends.

TELL STORIES THAT
BRING THEOLOGY TO LIFE

Nearly every sermon that gives priority to systematic theology should contain at least one real-life story that brings theology to life.[16] A story not only makes the sermon interesting, but also adds to the credibility to the claim of the sermon by showing that the claim is true. It also helps the congregation members recognize that the theological point relates directly to their everyday worlds. Furthermore, by entering into the story, the community often experiences the significance of the doctrinal or theological point.

Charles R. Blaisdell, Regional Minister of the Christian Church (Disciples of Christ) in Northern California and Nevada, tells the following story in a sermon on the priesthood of all believers. Blaisdell defines a priest as "one who shows God to other people" and urges the members of the congregation to be priests:

> Let me tell you a story that happened in an urban church a few years ago. As a downtown, urban church, the congregation was accustomed to having all kinds of folks happen in on Sunday morning. One Sunday morning, a fellow came in late; a big guy, obviously disturbed, sort of dangerous-looking. He took a seat down in front (because, of course, none of the church members were sitting there).
>
> At one point in the service, the man stood up, all 6-plus feet of him, and he began moaning and gesturing and sobbing and shouting, all at the same time. Except for him, the church was dead still for a moment.
>
> Then, from one of the back pews, 80-year-old Madeline stood up, all four-foot-eleven of her, and she walked down to where the man was now standing. Madeline—who for more than fifty years had led mission, studied and chaired women's circles, and served as a deacon and an elder and tenaciously taught that congregation about faith. And she

did so again that morning. She taught us all something about what it means to be a bearer of God's grace.

She came and stood beside that man. She reached up and put her arm around him, and gently sat him down beside her, and for the rest of the service you could barely hear her saying, "Shush. There. There. Shh. There. There," as she held him and rocked him like a baby.[17]

Blaisdell then interprets Madeline's actions that morning as priestly. The preacher urges the congregation to engage in similar "priesting."

Biography and autobiography are especially important sources of stories. When the preacher narrates how a person came to a particular theological insight, the congregation members often identify with aspects of the story. As they hear the narrative, they experience it via their own imaginations. For instance, when we hear the story of how James Cone came to articulate his distinctive approach to African American theology, the congregation imaginatively identifies with the ravages of racism in the United States and develops a tacit understanding of why the motif of liberation is central to that theology. As I point out below, these qualities intensify when preachers tell their own stories.

SUGGEST CONNECTIONS BETWEEN THEOLOGY AND THE EVERYDAY WORLD

The preacher can help the congregation make connections between elements of doctrine (and systematic theology) and life.[18] A key question is, what are the implications for the community and the wider world of the sermon's theological position? Given the lack of theological agility in many congregations, I tend to think that the preacher usually needs to make a direct statement about these implications and give examples of how they play out. However, some circumstances will call for the homily to take a more indirect approach that allows the congregation members to draw things out for themselves.

To take an example, Teresa Stricklen, now professor of preaching at Pittsburgh Theological Seminary but previously a pastor, connects the doctrine of the Trinity directly to Trinity Presbyterian Church in Nashville, Tennessee.

> Today is Trinity Sunday, a time when we talk Trinity. Many pastors dread Trinity Sunday. They hope it falls on a Memorial Day weekend or graduation Sunday, even Mother's Day—anything so they don't have to talk about the Trinity. After all, what is the Trinity anyway? And what good is it? Well, despite the perils, we are going to talk Trinity today. After all, how can a church called Trinity Presbyterian NOT talk about the Trinity?[19]

This beginning suggests a connection to the congregation. The sermon overviews materials in the Bible that some in the church have taken to be seeds of Trinitarianism, and recalls important moments in the formation of the doctrine of the Trinity.

Stricklen then moves to the heart of the sermon: "What's the Trinity got to do with us in the twenty-first century?" She lifts up two points at which Trinitarianism has immediate impact on the congregation. For one, the Trinity "keeps our technologized lives dynamically alive, responsive to the deep, fluid mysteries of life in God." Day to day, we often think that we are in "a Dilbert world." We "get into our cars and turn the key, expect them to run us wherever we want to go. We push a button, and computers rule the day." The Trinity is a kind of "dancing divinity" reminding us "that the important things in life cannot be quantified, scheduled, controlled." She helps the congregation members identify moments when they can live into the great mystery.

Second, the Trinity teaches us what it means to be created in the image of God. The image of God is inherently relational since that image is inherently Trinitarian. To be an individual in God is simultaneously to give ourselves to live in communion with others. "In the Trinity, we see individuality in community." This perspective challenges the "rugged me-first individualism that characterizes much of life at the beginning of the twenty-first century" by offering an alternative vision of the "Christian notion of personhood that lives in a dynamic relationship with others, offering unique individual gifts to God for the common good in such a way that individuality is not lost but enhanced in its blending with others' gifts, like musical instruments all coming together in a grand symphony." The sermon then points out circumstances in life when such individuality-in-community makes an everyday difference.

DEAL SERIOUSLY WITH QUESTIONS

Some questions that people have about systematic theology are informational. An example would be, "What does supralapsarianism mean?" Other questions have to do with how to respond to particular theological claims. For example, Christian tradition holds that the true church is identified by four marks: one, holy, catholic, apostolic. Given the oneness of the church, is it necessary for African American Christians, European American Christians, and Christians of other groups to disband the current configurations of most congregations and denominations along racial and ethnic lines and to reconvene congregations as multicultural entities? Still other questions cut close to the existential nerve of the church in a different way by raising questions of meaning: "What can I believe about God's love given the fact that my child is dying of leukemia?"

Preachers need to demonstrate in the sermon that they have heard such questions from the congregation and deal with them in a serious way.[20] The preacher often needs to explore different ways of answering the questions and critically evaluate the various possibilities. Simple answers seldom satisfy such questioners. Laypeople often think that a preacher is shallow if he or she offers a shortcut answer to a long and difficult question.

From time to time, the preacher needs to encourage the congregation to raise questions about some of its beliefs, especially when those beliefs do not appear adequate. Raising questions is also often a way to provoke curiosity and to set in motion explorations that result in persons arriving at new places of understanding.

R. Robert Cueni, pastor of a congregation in Kansas City that has a large number of highly educated people, begins a sermon on "Can We Be Certain?" by naming some important questions:

> As a people of faith, how can we be certain that what we believe is true? Given the diversity of human community, how can we be sure about the claims of Christianity? Given the competing claims of the sacred texts of other world religions, what makes us think that the Bible is a trustworthy revelation of God? Given the uncertainty of history, how do we know that Jesus really lived? Given the empirical claims of science, can we be certain that God even exists?[21]

Congregational members in study groups, pastoral calling, and parking-lot conversation had raised most of these questions. Their vocalization in the sermon signals the congregation that the pastor heard the members and may prompt some listeners to ask these queries for themselves for the first time.

Cueni points out that "we cannot be absolutely certain" that Christianity is true according to the standards of Enlightenment science and philosophy. As an alternative way of thinking, the preacher shows how a theological formulation from the past can be helpful today. "We first believe and then we see the evidence that confirms what we believe. Consider the motto of the eleventh-century monk, Saint Anselm: *Credo ut intelligam.* 'I believe so that I might understand.' Notice that Anselm argues that belief precedes understanding, not the other way around." We do not become certain (in the sense of having incontrovertible proof), but we can reach a place at which believing makes sense.

NAME YOUR OWN CONVICTIONS

As a general rule, it is good for preachers to name their own theological convictions forthrightly in the sermon. Not only is this disclosure a matter of integrity, but many people want to know where the pastor stands, and why, so they can dialogue with him or her around matters of theological importance.

Beyond simply naming their own beliefs, ministers can often reconstruct the process of theological discovery through which they arrived at their beliefs. By telling of their own journeys, they can create a bond between themselves and the congregation, as people recognize their own struggles. This telling can also teach the congregation, through example, how laity can think their way through theological questions.

For example, in a sermon on the second coming of Jesus in the so-called "little apocalypse" of Mark 13, I sketched the historical circumstances of the Markan community: the temple destroyed, the ground still wet from the blood of war with Rome, conflict between the Christian Jewish community of Mark and conventional Jewish people, economic deprivation, social turmoil, fear of the future. The community believed that it was living in the great tribulation that was to precede the return of Jesus from heaven to end this world and to create a new one. I explained that belief in the second coming was a way of making hopeful sense of such distressing circumstances:

> It is one thing to understand the point of this passage in its first-century context. It is another to press the question, "Do I . . . do you . . . believe that God will intervene in history in a singular moment of cosmic transformation when God will end this world and give birth to a new one?"
>
> I have to say, with absolute frankness, that I do not anticipate such a day. I do have a very strong sense of God

working toward a better future, but not through an apocalyptic cataclysm.[22]

The sermon then articulates three reservations about the view
that God will interrupt history. First, the divine integrity is com-
promised if God has the power to end suffering and yet allows
the suffering of the world not only to continue but multiply. Second, Mark presumes a model of a three-story universe that we
no longer share. Third, Mark operates with a notion that God
has unlimited power and can do anything at any time. However,
if God is omnipotent and does not end the suffering of the world,
then we can longer believe that God is unconditional love.

The sermon then posits an alternative understanding of the
second coming based on the distinction between surface witness and deeper witness articulated in chapters 3 and 4, above.
The deeper witness of the text reminds us that God is not satisfied with the world the way it is. God wills blessing for all and
is working through present historical circumstances to lure the
world toward such a state. Sometimes present social realities
must be dismantled in order for more just social worlds to
emerge. While I do not believe that God is omnipotent, I
believe God has more power than any other entity and that
God's power is inexhaustible. Transformation is not a steady
march of progress, as if the world is getting better and better
every day in every way, but more like a spiral.

At times, of course, pastors may want to hold in abeyance a
public statement of their convictions on a particular subject.
This may be pastorally wise when the congregation is emotionally divided over an issue, or beginning to consider an issue. The
premature interjection of the pastor's opinion might polarize the
community or cause the community to prejudge the issue. Also,
as noted above, ministers can frequently use the process of theological reasoning by which they came to their conclusion as a
means-of-teaching moment for the congregation.

As a young pastor I was hesitant to state clearly what I
believed, especially when my beliefs were not shared by many
members of the congregation. However, when I took a deep

breath and articulated my convictions, people typically had three reactions. First, they respected this demonstration of integrity. Second, many people expressed genuine interest in why I thought as I did. Third, a few people recognized that, at an intuitive level, they shared similar convictions but had not named or owned them.

EMBODY THE SERMON
IN AN ENGAGING WAY

A generation ago, we often spoke of "delivery" as a dimension of preaching, by which we meant the use of the voice and the body in the act of preaching. That term is now rightly supplanted by "embodiment." The language of "embodiment" calls attention to the fact that the minister and the sermon are conjoined in the moment of preaching. The pastor does not simply deliver a message to the congregation in the same way that the driver of an airfreight delivery truck delivers an overnight letter to an office. Preachers bring the sermon to life through their whole beings.

I have noticed a peculiar phenomenon with respect to embodiment. Preachers are often relatively subdued when talking overtly about doctrine or theology (or even about biblical exegesis) than in other parts of the sermon. They are typically much more animated when telling a story or talking about contemporary issues. This energy differential has two negative effects. First, it suggests to the congregation that direct talk about theology or the Bible is not as important as stories or other contemporary matters. Second, the lower level of intensity makes it easy for the congregation's attention to wander.

Consequently, the preacher needs to maintain a consistent energy level to signal the importance of all of the material when embodying a sermon that is altogether focused on doctrine or theology, or when embodying parts of a sermon that directly deal with doctrinal and theological matters. At the same time, the preacher should embody the sermon in ways that are consistent with its theological content. If the preacher is truly excited about the claim of the sermon, then the sermon itself should come to life in the pulpit with excitement. If the sermon is more sober or exploratory, then the preacher should speak and act in the pulpit in ways that are more sober and questioning.

Theology can be exciting when the preacher is passionate, uses language that is accessible to the congregation, and helps listeners catch the significance of the doctrine or theological reflection for the world. While these things are not a formula for successful communication, they usually help create a preaching ethos in which the congregation has an optimum opportunity to enter the world of the sermon.

6

Integrating Systematic Theology
into the Preaching Calendar

Physical fitness teachers remind us that we need to eat and exercise in balanced ways. Too many chocolate chip cookies and not enough broccoli leaves us malnourished. Too many exercises of one muscle group and not enough of another can cause the body to malfunction. The human body is a system in which all parts must work together for good health.

In 1 Corinthians 12:12–26 the apostle Paul compares the Christian community to a human body. As the term "system" implies, systematic theology is also a system in which the various elements must work together to develop a healthy congregational body. The essential elements of theology need to become a part of the congregation's diet and exercise plan. Preachers and congregations sometimes favor certain aspects of theology while ignoring others, thus leading to theological malnourishment. Without a full range of theological exercise, my spouse says, a congregation can "get a kink in its theological soul."[1]

This chapter first considers ways that the minister can integrate the full range of systematic theology into preaching from a selected lectionary. We then explore similar possibilities for preaching based on free selection of text, doctrine, or element of systematic theology.

SYSTEMATIC THEOLOGY
AND A SELECTED LECTIONARY

The word "lectionary" indicates a list of passages for reading from the Bible. Churches use two kinds of lectionaries. A continuous lectionary (*lectio continua*) is one in which the readings follow sequentially from a single book (or series of books) in the Bible, so that a pastor might preach through Romans. In a selected lectionary (*lectio selecta*), the readings are selected from different parts of the Bible. The Revised Common Lectionary, one of the most popular loci of preaching in the long-established denominations today, combines *lectio selecta* (during Advent-Christmas-Epiphany, and Lent-Easter-Pentecost) with the possibility of *lectio continua* (in Ordinary Time).

The lectionary is praised for a panorama of reasons.[2] It simplifies the choice of a text for the sermon and enables long-range planning for preaching and worship. More significantly, the lectionary exposes preacher and congregation to a wide range of texts from the Bible, and discourages the preacher from returning again and again to the same handful of passages. The discipline of following the lectionary is emblematic of following God.

Despite the lectionary's popularity among preachers, my impression is that few preachers think about the Christian year and the lectionary in connection with doctrine and systematic theology.[3] We need to give critical attention to this relationship. Systematic theology and the Christian year are not only different theological modes, but (depending on the content of a particular systematic theology) they sometimes fine tune theological visions differently. From the standpoint of some systematic theologies, the theology of the Christian year does not fully represent Christian vision and concern, and even misrepresents some things.

As noted previously, systematic theology refers broadly to the attempt to make a logical, coherent, comprehensive interpretation of what a Christian community believes (or can believe) concerning essential elements of Christian faith and life. Systematic theology usually deals sequentially with the community's foundational beliefs, beginning with the topic of our awareness of God and continuing through Christ, the Holy Spirit, the church, the world, and eschatology.

By contrast, the Christian year articulates its theology in a narrative model in a liturgical setting. The Christian year tells the story of redemption through Jesus Christ in two great cycles of worship: Advent-Christmas-Epiphany, and Lent-Easter-Pentecost. Ordinary Time begins after Epiphany Day and lasts until Ash Wednesday, resuming after Pentecost and going through Christ the Cosmic Sovereign. Of particular interest for this book is the fact that each of the major seasons is governed by a doctrinal or theological motif. While the Christian year and the lectionary lift up theological themes that are crucial to the community of faith, they do not incorporate the comprehensiveness or linear clarity of systematic theology.

The lectionary readings have been chosen to illumine the doctrines or aspects of a season's theology. From the standpoint of the Christian year, preachers need to be aware that their assignment is not simply to preach from the Bible but to relate the text to the main theological themes of the season and the day.

The following list summarizes the major theological themes of the seasons and the roles of the Bible readings.

Advent. The main theological themes of Advent are eschatology and recognition of Jesus Christ as agent of redemption who will complete the manifestation of the realm of God—that great time when all relationships and circumstances will fully reflect God's purposes. The first Sunday in Advent continues the eschatological motif of the last Sundays of the Christian year by concentrating on the apocalyptic consummation of history at the second coming of Jesus Christ. The fact that the Christian year begins and ends with eschatological vision reminds the congregation that its present life is to prepare for (and witness to) the restored world that God is bringing. The preacher is to use the Bible readings to initiate conversation with the congregation regarding what we believe concerning the second coming and to help the community prepare for it. As the calendar draws nearer to Christmas, the emphasis shifts from the second coming to the first. The pastor uses the lections to help the congregants to recognize the significance of the first coming of Jesus Christ, especially to recognize the significance and continuing effect of his first Advent, and to respond accordingly (e.g., through repentance, testimony, and trust) in the recognition that redemption is not complete after the first Advent but awaits the second.

Christmas. The preeminent theological emphasis for Christmas Day and the following Sundays is redemption through Jesus Christ, particularly the role of incarnation in redemption. The Christian year calls for the preacher to interpret the Bible texts so as to explore how they bring focus to our understanding of redemption and incarnation.

Epiphany. Epiphany is a day rather than a season. Its leading theme is the manifestation of God's grace through Jesus Christ for gentiles. Gentiles come to know the saving presence of the God of Israel, and God welcomes them into the eschatologically restored world.

Ordinary Time (from Epiphany to Lent). In Ordinary Time, the church meditates on the redemptive significance of Jesus Christ for the everyday world. What are the effects of the first Advent? How does the magnetic field of the second Advent reach into our day-to-day thoughts, feelings, and actions as Christians? In this short segment of Ordinary Time, the preacher would use the readings from the Bible to amplify the themes of Epiphany as well as to emphasize growth in discipleship.

Lent. The main doctrinal and theological theme of Lent is the ministry of Jesus Christ as divine agency whose appearance marks the movement toward the final manifestation of the realm of God with particular attention to the role of the cross. The preacher refracts the Bible readings through these themes. For example, what tempts us (as Jesus was tempted) to turn away from the realm of God? As Lent climaxes in Holy Week, the readings increasingly focus on the cross as the preacher must confront the question of Jesus' death in the manifestation of divine rule. Lent has historically been a period when the church prepares candidates for baptism, thus opening the homiletical door for a recollection of the congregation's theology of baptism.

Easter. The main doctrinal and theological theme of Easter is the resurrection of Jesus as the definitive demonstration of the presence of the realm of God. The readings after Easter help the community identify the effects of that presence in the midst of this world of principalities and powers. Other doctrinal emphases associated with Easter are the providence of God for faithful witnesses and the resurrection of the dead.

Pentecost. Like Epiphany, Pentecost is a day and not a season. From the point of view of the Christian year, the season of resurrection (Easter) ends with the giving of the Holy Spirit to the church not only to sustain the church as it awaits the second coming, but to empower the church for witness (especially the mission to the gentiles and conflicts around it). The doctrine of the Holy Spirit is obviously the central theological element. The preacher probes how the biblical readings for the day of Pentecost intersect with the church's teaching of the Spirit.

Ordinary Time (from Trinity Sunday through Christ the Cosmic Sovereign). The comments above about Ordinary Time pertain here, calibrated for the resurrection and the empowering presence of the Spirit. This Time begins with the doctrine of the Trinity and includes the communion of saints (in connection with All Saints' Day) and eschatology as in Advent. The Revised Common Lectionary provides two sets of readings from the First Testament and the Psalms for each Sunday in Ordinary Time. One set coordinates with the gospel lesson, while the other set functions as a modified form of continuous reading and introduces a number of theological themes outside the main themes of

Ordinary Time. In both the shorter and longer sectors of Ordinary Time, some of the options for Bible readings are arranged as *lectio continua*, thus making continuous exposition of scripture possible in preaching.

The interpretation of Christian vision created in the Christian year and the lectionary is quite powerful, for it is communicated from week to week in the practice of the congregation. As noted in chapter 2, practices are things that congregations do over time to form Christian identity and behavior.[4] The congregation members are sometimes consciously aware of what they learn to think, feel, and do as a result of Christian practice. For instance, people name the world in the language and concepts that they get from the Christian year and the lectionary. However, the congregation is sometimes affected intuitively and at the level of feeling by practice. By participating in worship, people develop a feel for the theological vision of the church year and the lectionary. Members may not be able to articulate all aspects of that vision easily, but the vision can be deeply embedded in the self and the community. The preacher needs to help the community reflect critically on both the conscious and intuitive results of the Christian year.

Theological Reservations about the Christian Year and a Selected Lectionary

From the perspective of systematic theology, four issues arise in connection with the theological vision and method of the Christian year and the lectionary.

1. While biblical scholars frequently note that the lectionary privileges certain parts of the Bible while neglecting others, even more important (and less noticed) is the fact that the Christian year does not bring the fullness of Christian doctrine or systematic theology into the consciousness of the congregation. James A. Sanders of the Claremont School of Theology notes of the lectionary and the Christian year, "A Christocentric hermeneutic focuses on God's work as redeemer almost exclusively," and he calls for a theocentric hermeneutic that "permits an understanding of all phases of God's work."[5]

Preachers who lionize the Christian year and the lectionary may think that the more than four hundred Bible readings over the course of the three-year lectionary give the preacher enough springboards to key aspects of Christian doctrine. Indeed, an exegetically and theologically alert preacher will ask of every text that appears in the lectionary, "What aspects of Christian doctrine does this text prompt us to consider?" Particularly in Ordinary Time, a text may lead preacher and people to an element of doctrine or theology outside the theological framework of the Christian year or the lectionary.

However, while the preceding possibilities may be true, the very structure of the Christian year (moving from Advent through Pentecost into Ordinary Time) does not give the congregation an opportunity to systematize its thinking in the manner of systematic theology. Hence, the congregation may never get a sense of its faith as a coherent whole except as it is summarized in affirmations of faith (that themselves need considerable interpretation). Even individuals and congregations who are deeply intuitive and resist linearity need periodically to catch the big picture and how its various parts relate so that they can reflect critically on them.

Along these lines, the preacher must monitor the doctrines and theological ideas that come to expression in preaching over the course of the Christian year. Very likely, the preacher will have to supplement the theological themes of the Christian year and the lectionary by developing series of sermons (and individual messages) that bring neglected aspects of doctrine and theology into the purview of the congregation. Because a singular theological perspective does not dominate Ordinary Time, the preacher can easily depart from the lectionary for series of sermons on doctrine or elements of systematic theology. The models discussed in the next section, "Free Selection of Text, Doctrine, or Theological Point," may help.

2. Many preachers have a propensity for theological eisegesis when encountering Bible passages in the context of the Christian year. That is, they predetermine the theological implications of the texts by reading from the perspective of the theological themes of the season or of the day. This phenomenon downplays

(and may even violate) the otherness of both biblical texts and doctrines (or elements of theology).

For instance, on Trinity Sunday, I repeatedly hear preachers read the fully developed Chalcedonian doctrine of the Trinity into the Bible readings. That mature doctrine is the product of reflection that took place after the period of the Second Testament. The Second Testament contains *seeds* that the later church interpreted as the origins of the doctrine of the Trinity, but that doctrine is not found in its complicated form in the Second Testament.[6]

The lectionary preacher need not always squeeze a text to make it fit the Christian year. Indeed, I earlier cited Arthur Van Seters to the effect that an encounter with the Bible "has the potential to explode the boundaries of doctrine."[7] A text can also explode (or implode) the boundaries of the Christian year. My observation, however, is that preachers tend to tame texts in accordance with the expectations of the Christian year.

3. The preacher must be critical of some of the underlying theological tendencies of the lectionary, for the Christian year and the lectionary actually exacerbate some problems in Christian theology. Shelley Cochran, whose Ph.D. dissertation deals with the hermeneutical presuppositions of the lectionary in the setting of the Christian year, points out that the Christian year and the lectionary are latently anti-Jewish. The seasonal categories of the Christian year are exclusively Christian. By structuring the Christian year exclusively on Jesus Christ, all things Jewish are made subordinate. The First Testament is typically limited to providing background for interpreting Christ and the church. The story of Israel is never heard in its own grand sweep. On a typical Sunday in the two major cycles, passages in the First and Second Testaments are related by means of a hermeneutic of prophecy and fulfillment. The results of such tendencies are particularly pernicious because they are not labeled in the Christian house nor are they frequently discussed by preachers, though they contribute to the anti-Judaism and anti-Semitism that continue to plague the church.[8]

4. The Christian year can lead to a disproportionate emphasis on Jesus Christ and relative neglect of God and the Holy Spirit. Just above, I cited James A. Sanders, who pleads for a

theocentric approach to preaching that "permits an understanding of all phases of God's work."

Not only are the two major cycles christological in focus, but the Bible readings in the lectionary in those seasons (and in one set of readings in Ordinary Time) presuppose that the gospel reading sets the theme for the day. While the preacher and the congregation can certainly reflect more broadly on God and the Holy Spirit in the Christian year and the lectionary, these liturgical frames do not provide sustained seasons for such considerations.

Indeed, the Christian year and lectionary revise the theological emphasis of the early church. The earliest Christian witnesses in the Second Testament see Jesus Christ and the church as revealing good news about *God*. In the strict sense, the earliest Christian is *theo*logical whereas the Christian year and the lectionary are *christo*logical. At the end of this chapter I mention two possibilities for supplementing or revisioning a calendric approach to preaching that would maintain a theological focus while accounting for christological elements that are essential to Christian faith.

FREE SELECTION OF TEXT, DOCTRINE, OR THEOLOGICAL POINT

Many pastors freely select the biblical texts or the topics for their sermons. That is, they choose a passage or a topic without reference to the lectionary. Typically such ministers make their selections based on their pastoral analysis of the congregation and its needs, although some preachers choose on the basis of their personal interests. Some pastors employ free selection in the context of the Christian year. They do not follow the lectionary, but they do choose texts or topics that relate to the seasons of the year. In Advent, for instance, a clergyperson might present a series of sermons on the coming of Christ. As I noted above, congregations that follow a lectionary sometimes depart from the lectionary in Ordinary Time in order to allow for sermons that focus directly on local needs or interests.

Free selection easily allows the preacher to bring systematic theology directly into the sermon. When *developing a single sermon that originates from the exposition of a biblical passage*, a pastor can always bring a text into the kind of theological conversation described in chapter 3. In fact, a preacher might select a particular biblical passage because it raises a theological theme that the congregation needs to consider. For example, in a year when civic elections are taking place, the preacher might turn to a passage in the Bible that depicts the responsibility of public officials. I think of Psalm 72 with its description of the sovereign of Israel as responsible for seeing that justice is mediated throughout the covenantal community. In that psalm (as in many passages in the Bible), the degree to which the community cares for the poor is an index of the degree to which public officials and other leaders are faithfully discharging their responsibility. The psalm can become an occasion for the preacher to reflect theologically on similarities and differences between the situation of the sovereign (and government) of Israel and public leadership today, as well as the degree to which Christians should support governmental systems and leaders that promote the care of the poor.

Preachers can also bring systematic theology overtly into messages when they develop *a series of sermons around a particular biblical theme, book, or character*. Again, a preacher might select biblical material that particularly addresses the situation in the congregation. For example, in a Christian community beset by personal animosity, a pastor might select a series of biblical passages that deal with forgiveness. Over the course of several Sundays, the preacher can explore the nature of forgiveness and its practice in church by bringing biblical texts into dialogue with a theology of forgiveness in the context of the circumstances of the congregation.

A congregation can also *follow the Christian year without following a lectionary*. That is, a congregation can observe the seasons of Advent, Christmas, Epiphany, Lent, Easter, and Pentecost without following the lectionary readings prescribed for those seasons. The preacher could then either select Bible readings to help interpret the seasons of the year or develop sermons that start and move as systematic theology.[9] In Lent, for example, the preacher could develop a series that unfolds a theological understanding of the cross.

The preacher can also develop *individual sermons that start and move as systematic theology*. For example, when Westminster Presbyterian Church in Wilmington, Delaware, rededicated its sanctuary on Reformation Sunday after an extensive renovation, the pastor, Jon M. Walton, took advantage of the occasion to preach a sermon titled "Still Presbyterian after All These Years." In a winsome fashion, and with tasteful humor, Walton recalls the history and essential beliefs of the Presbyterian movement, telling the story of the Reformation and Calvin's role in it, as well as the emergence of the major confessions and the distinctive theological qualities of Presbyterianism. Walton explains why he has self-consciously chosen to remain a Presbyterian. This church lives day by day (and even moment by moment) with a deep trust in the gracious sovereignty of God, approaches the scriptures in a thoughtful manner, worships in a simple and intelligent way, honors preaching, emphasizes education (especially learning to interpret the divine presence in all of life) in the Christian community and in the broader world, trusts the gifts and leadership of its laypeople, has the courage to name and correct its theological and ethical errors, and continues to join with Jesus in witnessing to the realm of God in both personal and public spheres.[10]

A preacher can also develop a *series of sermons that start and move as systematic theology*. I have suggested that each year a preacher should develop *several connected messages that summarize the foundational theological convictions of the congregation and the denomination or movement with which it is in covenant*. Such a series both orients newcomers and refreshes the memories of established members. For instance, in congregations who subscribe to the Nicene Affirmation of Faith, preachers often develop a series on each article of the affirmation. Such a series might look like this:

Sermon 1: We Believe in One God
Sermon 2: We Believe in One Lord, Jesus Christ
Sermon 3: We Believe in the Holy Spirit

Each message offers a theological interpretation of the significance of the affirmation that is the focus of that message. The series could be expanded, of course, to take more detailed account of the various articles of the affirmation of faith.

A preacher can similarly outline a similar series *based on the categories of systematic theology*. I illustrate with the divisions of Clark M. Williamson's *Way of Blessing, Way of Life*, a theology describing Christian faith as a path to blessing and life:[11]

> Sermon 1: Blessing, Life, and Conversation: Thinking
>   Theologically
> Sermon 2: The Direction of the Way: Revelation
> Sermon 3: Light for the Path: Scripture and Tradition
> Sermon 4: God the Creator and Redeemer of Life
> Sermon 5: Creation, Providence, and Evil
> Sermon 6: Neighbors Along the Way: Humanity
> Sermon 7: Jesus Christ: Pioneer of Our Faith
> Sermon 8: The Spirit of New Life
> Sermon 9: Companions on the Way: The Church
> Sermon 10: Help for the Way: Preaching, Sacraments, and
>   Ministry
> Sermon 11: The Goal of the Way

Each sermon would summarize the essential convictions concerning that topic.

The preacher can also develop *a series of sermons that interprets one article of the affirmation or systematic theology*. This approach allows the congregation to explore the article with more precision. For instance, in a congregation that confesses the United Church of Christ Statement of Faith, a preacher can develop a series of sermons on each of the clauses in the article that deals with the church. The congregation states, "You [God] call us into your church:"

> Sermon 1: to accept the cost and joy of discipleship
> Sermon 2: to be your servants in the service of others
> Sermon 3: to proclaim the gospel to all the world
> Sermon 4: to resist the powers of evil
> Sermon 5: to share in Christ's baptism and eat at his table
> Sermon 6: to join [Christ] in passion and victory

Each sermon would focus on a single aspect of ecclesiology.

The preacher can also take a more revisionary approach to interpreting such an article or affirmation. For example, modeling the kind of thinking required to bring systematic theology in the sermon, Rebecca Button Prichard, in *Sensing the Spirit: The Holy Spirit in Feminist Perspective*, uses categories from sensual experience to explore ways in which we encounter the presence and movement of the Holy Spirit.[12] We experience the Spirit through sound, sight, touch, taste, and smell. Categories in this pneumatology of the senses discussed by this systematic theologian and preacher suggest focuses for a series on the Spirit:

Sermon 1: The Spirit and sound (breath: spirit, speech, silence)
Sermon 2: The Spirit and sight (vision, verdure, viridity)
Sermon 3: The Spirit and taste (desire, denial, delight)
Sermon 4: The Spirit and touch (feeling, fire, fervor)
Sermon 5: The Spirit and smell (aroma, odor, adoration)

In each case, Prichard traces biblical passages, images, and themes that contribute to the study, identifies voices (especially but not exclusively feminist) in the history of the church that address the topic, brings the theme into conversation with contemporary systematic theology, and offers her own provocative and often profoundly moving interpretation. A congregation that participates in this series will become attuned to ways in which it experiences the Spirit in the everyday world of the senses.

A preacher can also develop a series of sermons around *issues that are alive in the congregation*,[13] each sermon addressing a different essential aspect of the issue. For example, through pastoral listening, R. Robert Cueni discovered the need for a series on "Questions of Faith for the Inquiring Believer." Cueni focused each sermon around a different question that was important to people in the congregation:[14]

Sermon 1: Why Do Good People Do Bad Things?
Sermon 2: Can We Be Certain [about what we believe]?
Sermon 3: What about Evangelism?

Sermon 4: Where Is God when Bad Things Happen to Good People?

Sermon 5: How Do We Live with Our Differences?

Sermon 6: What about the Trinity?

Sermon 7: For What Do We Pray?

Sermon 8: What Are Christians Supposed to Do?

Sermon 9: What Is So Important about Going to Church?

Sermon 10: Must Religion and Science Conflict?

Sermon 11: If Christ Is the Answer, What Is the Question?

In each sermon, the preacher explores the nature of the question itself, and responds to the question on the basis of answers that are informed by the theology of the preacher in dialogue with the Bible, the denomination, and systematic theologians.

James A. Sanders has proposed an alternative lectionary year that includes the telling of the story of the First Testament in sequence.[15] The congregation could thereby follow the story of Israel in its grand sweep both for its own sake and to provide a narrative context for the story of Jesus and the early church. In a similar way, the church could create a preaching calendar based on the categories of systematic theology. The themes of the calendar would move across a year of preaching from our perception of God through the leading themes of the doctrines of God, Christ, Holy Spirit, Church, and World.

A preacher needs regularly to make sure that the full range of the congregation's convictions comes to expression in the pulpit. As I noted earlier, pastors must monitor the doctrines and theological themes and categories that are surfacing in sermons and those that are relatively muted and adjust accordingly. To be sure, a certain season of a congregation's life may call for a certain theological emphasis, but in order for the community to be a healthy theological body, a full theological regimen is as necessary as a full complement of vitamins and exercise for the human body.

7

Sample Sermons

In this chapter, I include two of my sermons that draw overtly on systematic theology. The first sermon originates from the interpretation of a biblical text, Acts 1:6–11. The other sermon starts and moves as systematic theology. Each sermon is annotated to provide the reader with an understanding of the role of systematic theology in the sermon and of qualities that I hope help theology come alive.

A SERMON ON THE ASCENSION OF JESUS

[I began the preparation of this sermon by identifying the theological claims of Acts 1:6–11 in the historical context of the Gospel of Luke and the book of Acts. My examination revealed a number of themes, including the relationship between Israel and the church, the relationship between the ascension and Pentecost, the Holy Spirit empowering the church's witness to the realm of God, the gentile mission taking place under divine aegis, the movement of the narrative of Acts from Jerusalem through Judea and Samaria to the ends of the earth, and the apocalyptic second coming of Jesus.[1] A single sermon cannot do justice to so many interpretive layers, and so I focused on the ascension as a demonstration of the sovereignty of Jesus over all other authorities, especially those that resist the realm of God. I traced the role of the ascension in theologians in the past, particularly the

*Reformers and Alexander Campbell, a moving spirit of my denomi-
nation—the Christian Church (Disciples of Christ).[2] I also consulted
contemporary systematic theologians Paul Tillich and Clark
Williamson, who represent the revisionary stream in which I think.
For perspectives outside my customary theological conversation partners, I turned to Christopher Morse and Karl Barth. After a brief
beginning intended to focus the sermon, the movement of the message
largely follows the flow of historical development: from the exegesis of
the text through considering the text in Christian tradition to contemporary systematic theology with practical pastoral implications.]*

Not long ago, we discussed the ascension in a class I teach
on Luke–Acts. Somehow the discussion turned to how the
class members visualize this scene. One of the students
with a background in the arts recalled a painting of an
ethereal Jesus in a white, diaphanous robe levitating from
earth to heaven. She said that she could hear a pipe organ
playing solemnly in the background. Another student
described an animated version, "kind of like the Simpsons." Still another imagined the ascension as watching
someone shoot up the atrium of a downtown hotel in a
glass elevator trimmed with lights.

*The sermon now considers the text from the categories of surface and
deeper witness (pp. 55–56).*

However, Karl Barth, a leader of the church in a previous
generation, is right. "There is no sense in trying to visualize the ascension in a literal event like going up in a bal-
loon."[3] For the story of the ascension in Acts 1 makes use
of first-century images and ideas that we no longer share.
For instance, they thought of the world as similar to a
three-story building with the earth in the middle, heaven
above, and an underworld below. We think of the universe
as infinitely expanding. It's hard for Jesus to arrive at the
edge of the universe if that edge never stops moving. We
know that a cloud cannot hold a human body in mid-air.
As for angels (the figures in white) materializing in the sky

making Barbara Walters–like interpretive remarks, well, if someone reported such a sight in one of my classes, I would gently recommend an appointment at the counseling center.

Barth, though, and many other biblical scholars and theologians, indicate that Luke uses first-century imagery to make a point that is not limited to a three-story universe. "Heaven" is a first-century way of speaking of the presence of God. To people in antiquity, heaven is the power center of the cosmos. The cloud is a First Testament way of describing God's presence and activity. Later in the book of Acts, and several other places in the Second Testament, the ascended Jesus is described as being "at the right hand of God." With apologies to left-handed people, I report that in the world of the Bible, the right hand is a position of authority. This expression is a first-century way of saying that Jesus is God's primary agent.

The sermon next summarizes the theological witness of the text and its importance for the social context of the book of Acts.

Put these things together, and we get the picture of Jesus as cosmic CEO. Since Jesus ascends to the very presence of God, we know two things: (1) Jesus can continue the work of restoring persons and communities that began during the earthly ministry, and (2) Jesus is more powerful than any other ruler in the world.

These affirmations are particularly important in the social world of the church in Acts. The church, of course, continues the witness to the restoration. But other leaders resist this witness. In the book of Acts, religious and political authorities often harass the early missionaries. For Stephen, harassment eventuates in death by stoning. Three times early Christians get thrown into jail. Luke leaves literary clues in the story of Paul to let us know that the Romans put the great missionary traveler to death.

Can you feel the impact of the story of the ascension in Luke's world of chaos, suffering, and death? Jesus is sovereign over all sovereigns of the earth. No matter what earthly rulers and authorities do to you, they do not have the last word. You can continue to witness to God's love for all and God's will for justice for all in the confidence that your witness is under the aegis of God.

Someone puts it this way: "Is Christianity simply the news that Christ died and then was alive again?" No. Christ "rose to *ascend*. Christ ascends to *reign*."[4] We get excited about Easter. But notice: this season of the Christian year begins with Easter but *climaxes* with the ascension. And the ascension makes Pentecost possible.

In the material that follows, the sermon moves beyond the text to consider how the text is understood in the Christian tradition, with particular attention to the emphases of the denomination in which it was preached.

This theme was so important to the early church that they gathered it up, combined it with some other references from the Second Testament, and put it in the Apostolic Affirmation of Faith.[5] "I believe in Jesus Christ . . . ascended into heaven, and . . . seated at the right hand of [God.]"

Martin Luther and John Calvin summarize the teaching of the church along these lines when they say that the notion that Jesus is seated at the "right hand of God" is an ancient saying that means that God is everywhere.[6] Paul Tillich, an almost contemporary Christian thinker, expands on this notion as the power of God "working everything in everything" with the goal of actualizing the realm of God in every relationship, and every circumstance.[7] There never is a moment when God is not at work for your good and for the good of all.

Our own ancestor Alexander Campbell contributes a memorable expression. The ascension enables Jesus to be the "administrator" of the realm of God.[8] From the right hand of power, Jesus is the active agent who brings the realm of God to expression in the everyday world.

A side note. Campbell's perception challenges my view of administration, especially when I am the one who has to do it. Paper pushing. Tending to details. Figuring out creative ways to get people to say "Yes" to jobs they really do not want, and then crabbing at them to do the jobs they do not want. How different to think of administration as responding to the ascended Jesus to do my part in facilitating the realm of God in everyday affairs. I can witness to the realm of God each time I write an e-mail.

The message now reaches its destination: the significance of the story of the ascension in contemporary systematic theology.

Clark Williamson and Christopher Morse, conteporary systematic theologians, pose a positive and negative pole for understanding the ascension. *The positive pole.* Williamson says, "The doctrine of the ascension [is] the most political of all doctrines."[9] It is political in the sense that for Christians, Jesus Christ is the final authority, and Jesus' will is always for unconditional love and unremitting justice. In every relationship. In every situation.

The negative pole. Morse, who teaches at Union Theological Seminary in New York, points that every affirmation of the church gives birth to things the church cannot affirm. Belief in the ascension commits the church to disbelieve any confession or any idea, and to disavow any action, that does not assert God's love and justice for all.[10]

The unconditional love and the universal will for justice of the ascended Christ stands over every Caesar. Sometimes that Caesar is a boss, a teacher, a drug, a drink, a parent, even a minister. It can be a system, such as racism, or even a congregation. The ascended Jesus stands over such situations and says "No," and works to bring about circumstances of love and justice.

When the church is faithful, it stands with Jesus, and seeks to find more loving and just ways. From time to time, as in the Acts of the Apostles, that witness brings

the church into conflict. Sometimes local Caesars seem
to prevail. But no matter, the church sees something the
local Caesars do not: Jesus ascended to heaven at the hand
of God.

*As the sermon concludes, I offer an image that I hope brings the the-
ology of the ascension to life and that helps the congregation perceive
implications of the ascension for their everyday worlds.*

I was chuckling a few moments ago over some of the ways
that members of my class on Luke–Acts tried to visualize
the ascension. Levitating in a diaphanous robe. As a character from the Simpsons. Riding toward heaven in a light-
rimmed elevator. But we had one more. An African
American recalled a mural painted with bold, rough figures on the side of a deteriorating ghetto building. At the
bottom: people standing unemployed on the street corner,
others asking for handouts, selling drugs, fighting, in jail.
On one side of the mural is a storefront church, the pastor directing people out the doors and into the streets.
One Christian is standing between a woman and a man
who is abusing her. Another church member is trying to
go with an addict into a hospital, but the hospital is turning them away because the addict has no insurance. So, the
helper has stuck her foot in the hospital door and will not
let it close. Still another person from the congregation is
clubbed by a police officer for objecting to someone being
pulled over for Driving While Black. A Bible school class
is lying head to toe in front of a bulldozer about to destroy
low-cost housing. Another group is carrying pasteboard
boxes filled with their cash out of the bank and are pouring them in a big pile to establish a common pool. Over it
all, a giant stick-figure Jesus bends down with arms spread
wide to gather up everything and everyone below. That
description brought the class to silence.

    In what circumstance do you need to witness to the
realm of God? At home? On your street? In school? At the
workplace? In the congregation?

Sometimes, as in the Acts, your world turns to chaos when you demonstrate the love and justice of God. But no matter how bitter the conflict, you can always look up. Do you see it? Jesus . . . at the right hand of God. And I see that hand gathering its gentle strength around you.

A SERMON ON BAPTISM

[This sermon, from a series on the identity of my movement, the Christian Church (Disciples of Christ), focuses on the meaning of baptism. The message starts and moves as systematic theology. Although our church does not subscribe to a formal affirmation of faith, Disciples sometimes use the Preamble to the Design of the denomination as a theological summary. The sermon is a theological exposition of the affirmation regarding baptism from that document: "Through baptism into Christ, we enter into newness of life and are made one with the whole people of God."[11] Although this article in the Preamble focuses on newness of life and unity with the ecumenical community, these two images only partly reflect the understanding of baptism in our movement. During preparation I consulted the Bible dictionaries and commentaries for understandings of water symbolism in the ancient world and of Jewish water rites. I discovered that the Second Testament contains too many images and meanings of baptism to consider each one in a single sermon. I reviewed how the Christian tradition understands baptism, especially the Reformers, and the practice of believers' baptism by immersion—a characteristic of the Christian Church (Disciples of Christ). I took into account contemporary reflection on baptism on the part of the Disciples' Commission on Theology, as well as the wider ecumenical discussion of baptism represented by Baptism, Eucharist, and Ministry.[12] *The structure of the sermon follows this process.]*

Who are we as members of the Christian Church (Disciples of Christ)? What are we to do as a congregation? I have heard you asking these questions. This series of sermons is an initial response. As I pointed out in sermons in the previous two weeks, our guide is the Preamble to the Design of our church. Although the term "preamble" does not strike fire in the religious imagination, this statement summarizes some key beliefs in our movement. We began where the Preamble begins: with a Disciple understanding of Jesus Christ as heir of the living God and sovereign and savior of the world. In the second sermon we rejoiced in God as maker of heaven and earth who joins us in a covenant of love.

I define the topic clearly in the following paragraph and then provide a picture of the act of immersion for listeners who may not have witnessed such a baptism. I also hope that those who have been immersed will recollect their own baptisms and will refract the theology of the sermon with their experience of immersion. If the sermon were not part of a series (thus requiring a beginning that connects the individual message to the series) I would begin the homily with the description of the baptismal scene below, connect that scene to the Preamble, and then pose the question, "What does baptism mean to us?"

Today we open the file in the Preamble that says: "Through baptism into Christ, we enter into newness of life and are made one with the whole people of God." What does baptism mean to us, especially our practice of immersing believers?

I love it when we immerse. Although we cannot see the water from our pews, we can see light reflecting from the surface of the water and dancing on the beams over the Table and over much of the front part of the sanctuary. We hear the water rustle as the pastor and the candidates step into the pool in their white robes. The long white robes, the light shimmering on the water—it's almost a transfiguration. The pastor positions the candidate at a 90-degree angle, raises a hand over the candidate's head, and invokes the Trinity. "Chris, I now baptize you in the name of. . . ." The pastor grips the candidate's arm and back, and lowers the candidate into the water. When the pastor pulls the candidate to the surface of the water, the whole sanctuary is alive with the sound.

I now recall significant references to water from the First Testament and Judaism to bring the congregation into the world of water symbolism in which the early church practiced baptism and to imply continuities between Judaism and Christian use of water symbolism. In my brief recollection of immersion, I concentrate on the water because it is essential to the meaning of baptism.

Water was a multifaceted symbol in the First Testament. In Genesis 1, God makes the world from a vast primeval sea. Water is necessary for creation and life. Indeed, each person comes into the world through a womb filled with water. The breaking of the mother's water is the beginning of a new phase of life for the child. God provides water when Israel is parching in the wilderness. Water makes arid ground fertile. When dishes and clothes and wounds and people are dirty, we wash them. Water comes to represent religious cleansing. Water renews. On a hot day, what is more refreshing than a glass of cool water? At the same time, water brings to mind chaos and death. When the earth was a cesspool of sin, God sent rain for forty days and nights to return the earth to chaos. Yet water is also salvation for Noah, for the ark floated on the water even as the flood drowned every living thing below.[13]

By the first century of the Common Era (the time of Jesus and the early church), the Jewish community performed a rite for gentiles similar to baptism as a part of conversion to Judaism. You've heard of the Dead Sea Scrolls? The people who wrote them lived at a place called Qumran, and practiced a form of immersion. John the Baptist and some other Jewish groups practiced baptism for another reason. They believed that the present age of history is so far from the divine purposes that God would destroy it in an apocalyptic cataclysm and create a new world in which all things reflect God's purposes. John pleads with the crowds to prepare for this cataclysm by repentance and by becoming a part of a community awaiting the new age. The means of joining the new community? Immersion. The baptism of John is preparation for a new world.

The message now reviews leading ideas and images of baptism in the Second Testament to demonstrate the pluralism of early Christian understandings of immersion.

When I turned the pages to the Second Testament, I got a little surprise. This testament contains multiple understandings of baptism. Several of them pick up ideas from Judaism. Here is a sample. Baptism is participation in the death of Jesus (Mark 10:38–40 and parallels)

is a means of being born from above (or born anew or again) (John 3:4)

demonstrates repentance (Acts 2:38)

promises forgiveness of sin (e.g., Acts 2:38; 10:43, 48; 22:16)

is dying and rising with Christ to walk in newness of life (Rom. 6:1–14; Col. 2:12–15)

washes away sin (1 Cor. 6:11; Rev. 7:14; 22:14)

is to the church as the Exodus from Egypt was to the Jewish community: a dramatic demonstration of liberation from oppression (1 Cor. 10:1–4)

initiates us into a community of the new age (1 Cor. 12:12–13; Eph. 1:14–15)

establishes the unity of the church: all who are baptized are in one body (1 Cor. 12:12–13; Eph. 4:4–6)

is a means whereby we put on Christ (Gal. 3:27–29)

creates a community in which there is neither male nor female, Greek nor Jewish person, slave nor free (1 Cor. 12:12–13; Gal. 3:27)

is a seal that the Holy Spirit is present and at work for us (Acts 2:38; 2 Cor. 1:22; Eph. 1:14–15)

enlightens self and the community (Eph. 5:14)

is to the church as circumcision is to the Jewish people: a sign that we are claimed by God's grace and are called to witness to God's ways (Col. 2:11–12)

regenerates and renews (Titus 3:5)

sprinkles our hearts clean (Heb. 10:22; 1 Peter 3:21–22)

begins the journey that takes us from this shadowy world to heaven where we have unmediated access to God (Heb. 10:19–25)

saves us in the same way that the ark carried Noah over the flood (1 Pet. 3:21)

marks us for the Living God in this world in which so
many lesser gods would claim us (Rev. 7:2)

is the river of the water of life (Rev. 22:1–2)

These differences prompt a notable Bible scholar to com-
ment that we cannot just "add all the views together" to find
the understanding of baptism in the Second Testament.[14]

*The sermon now moves to the heart of the understanding of baptism
in the tradition of our movement. I try to give theology a human face,
especially when discussing the historical context of Alexander Campbell's teaching on immersion.*

Despite this fantasia of images, we can detect a unifying
theme: baptism is something that God does for us. That
thread is the key to our movement's thinking about baptism. Our church's understanding of baptism includes
biblical teaching, but goes beyond that to create an overarching picture of what happens in immersion.

As you know, the tendrils of the theological roots of our
denomination reach to the Reformation. The key word is
assurance. For both Martin Luther and John Calvin, baptism is an assurance that God gives the community. Luther
says, "The first point about baptism is the divine promise"
of forgiveness of sin and salvation.[15] Baptism is not a good
work. It does not justify in and of itself. God's grace does
that. Baptism *assures* believers that we are justified.

Calvin thinks of baptism as "an outward sign by which
[God] seals on our consciences the promise of [the divine]
good will towards us." Baptism is a "testimony of divine
grace towards us, confirmed by an outward sign."[16]

Similar themes percolate in our ancestors Alexander
Campbell and Barton Stone. To better understand their
teaching, we need to realize that their ministries took
place at a time of hot debate over the role of feeling and
experience in Christian life. Some of Campbell's contem-
poraries believed that in order to know that you had
proper standing before God, you had to feel something

extraordinary. Without a dramatic experience, you could not be sure that God has accepted you. Campbell rejected this view, claiming that it made God's work in our behalf dependent on our feeling. Instead, Campbell took a more objective view. Through baptism and the breaking of the loaf, God communicates God's love for you in a straightforward way. You may have some feeling in response, but the power of God's efforts in your behalf does not depend on whether you feel them. All you need to do is embrace what God has done. Baptism, says Campbell, is "a solemn pledge and formal assurance on the part of [God] to the church that God has forgiven all our offences."[17]

The sermon suggests the practical importance of baptism using statements that people in Disciples circles sometimes make, such as, "I am not worthy to be baptized."

When you are baptized you should have no doubt as to God's love for you. Do you feel unworthy? Sure. Do you think that you do not deserve it? Sure. Do you think that you do not live up to God's love for you? Sure. But that is just the point. We are not baptized because we are worthy, but because we are not. God uses immersion to impress the *fact* of God's love on us precisely because we do not deserve it.

Campbell prefers baptism by immersion both because it is the pattern of the earliest church and because it communicates God's blessing to the believer more fully than other modes of baptism. Indeed, in a memorable expression, he says that baptism is "a sort of embodiment of the gospel, a solemn expression of it all in a single act."[18]

Stone came to think similarly. Making an analogy from the First Testament he said, "Did the waters of the Jordan, into which Namaan [dipped] himself at the command of Elisha—Did these waters literally wash away his leprosy? Or was it not the power of God through this act of obedience?"[19] The water does not save, but it mediates to us the knowledge that God's grace and power have liberated us.

While we Disciples do not have an official authority to write the terms of our faith for us, we do have a Commission on Theology to help us sort out what we believe. This commission reaffirms the heart of the teaching of Campbell and Stone, but with this important emendation. While the commission agrees that believers' baptism by immersion is the most appropriate mode, it reminds us that immersion is not the exclusive mode of baptism. God can use sprinkling and pouring, even of infants, to affirm God's unconditional love.[20] The infant may not have a conscious memory of this event, but parents and church fill in their memories later.

God uses the water to assure us of God's good pleasure toward us and of God's promises of faithfulness. Baptism does not change our status before God. God's grace has already given us full standing with God. The water is for our benefit. It impresses on us the awareness of God's love and trustworthiness. When we agree to be baptized, we indicate our trust in God's promises and our willingness to walk in the divine ways. We do not emerge from the waters as fully developed Christians. The walk up the steps of the baptistery is a beginning, not a destination. When we place our bare feet in the water, we indicate our desire to enter into a lifelong process of growth in discipleship. The act of immersion demonstrates that God is with us at every step.

Luther recalled a holy woman, who, when confronted by the devil, would remember that she had been baptized, that is, she had already been taken out of the domain of Satan's power and placed in the dominion of God.[21] Try that, next time your boss wants you to do something unethical, or you feel that your world is collapsing or your congregation is about to take an action to protect its own interests while denying its responsibility to witness in the world beyond the parking lot. Remember your baptism. Remember that God loves you unconditionally and is at work even as you breathe for your good and for the good of the world.

Baptism takes advantage of the senses.[22] At one level, the water functions as a reminder, much like a sticky note.

It brings to mind the fact that you are gathered into God's grace and that God is at work for your benefit. But, at another level, the senses are not merely physical. The human self is a whole. Physical sensation is a part of a deeper network of knowledge within the body, much of it below the surface of consciousness.

One of my colleagues, J. Gerald Janzen, refers to these things as body memories that are stored within the self and that can be stirred powerfully even without our conscious awareness. The water of baptism brings forth and creates body memories that associate the experience of immersion with being in the womb and bursting forth into new birth, with the watery mark of the unconditional love of the Great Creator, with the connection of being joined with others in a single body of witness, with the sense that God carries us across the floods of this world, with the deep awareness that we die and rise with Christ— that the water becomes a symbolic tomb for the power of sin and death and that God lifts us out of the water with the great arms of new life. God works through these body memories day by day to touch us with the divine presence.

The sermon now concludes with an incident that expresses in narrative form the theology of baptism advocated in the sermon. I hope that this story helps bring the Disciples' theology of immersion to life.

The summer after I graduated from seminary, I was an interim minister in Wray, Colorado. Robert, nearly six feet tall and weighing 240 pounds, made a confession of faith and prepared for immersion. It did not occur to me to ask if he had a fear of water.

When he appeared at the edge of the baptistery, his eyes were big as pie plates, and he was trembling like a stalk of grain in the wind in the fields on the edge of town. I led him into the water and got him situated, raised my hand over his head, and pronounced the baptismal formula. I placed my hand over his mouth and nose, gripped his back, and plunged him beneath the cleansing flood.

Now, I went to an ecumenical seminary in which nearly everyone else was from churches that practice sprinkling. I had never been taught how to immerse. I did not know that one key is for me to hook my foot over one of the feet of the candidate to keep the candidate anchored solidly to the floor of the baptistery.

At that time, I wore chest waders into the water so that I could keep my clothes on while I performed the baptism. That way, when the immersion was finished, I could take off the waders and return quickly to the chancel to continue leading the service.

Robert was big. I am not. As soon as he hit the water he had a surge of energy. I bent to help him. The church building was erected when contractors often lined baptismal tanks with sheet metal. You could hear Robert's feet banging against the metal sides of the baptistery and echoing around the sanctuary. Boooooom.

He grabbed my neck and pulled me toward him so that the top of my waders went below the surface of the water. Glub. Glub. Glub. Do you know how fast waders can fill with water? And how much they weigh?

Robert grabbed me with one hand and the side of the baptistery with the other. I heaved him up. He threw the water off his face and breathed a huge sigh of relief. Then he looked up at me and said, ever so quietly, "Safe."

Isn't that the point? Isn't that just the point? God uses the water of immersion to say to us, "No matter what happens, you are safe with me."

I find that congregations often respond well to sermons whose movement follows the sequential historical development of doctrine from the Bible through church history into contemporary systematic theology. However, there is no exclusive way to preach systematic theology. Preachers can develop sermons in many different forms in accord with the nature of the theological content and its purpose in the congregational setting.[23]

Appendix
Relationships among Contemporary and Historic Theological Families

As I noted earlier, we can speak generally of two kinds of theological families: contemporary and historical. The four major contemporary families are revisionary, liberation, postliberal, and evangelical. These categories or orientations result from different perspectives on how to relate Christian tradition to the contemporary world. The eleven major historic families are listed in Table 1. They emerged as the church sought to relate Christian faith to insights and circumstances of the past. They have become distinct traditions that are passed (and adapted) from generation to generation.

As Table 1 shows, contemporary and historical theological families are often related. Most preachers bear marks of both contemporary and historic families. For instance, I am a Reformed theologian with a revisionary approach; while my basic theological content is Reformed, I handle that content in a revisionary manner.

In addition, we can observe different theological nuances in churches in different racial and ethnic communities. For instance, Baptist churches in European and African American communities share much common theology. Yet, some theological themes are often stronger in one community than in the other.

Table 1 lays out a scheme for relating contemporary and historical families, and is followed by thumbnail descriptions of these groups' families. You can plot your theological location on the chart as a way of getting a clear sense of your particular theological orientation and its implications for preaching. When you are cognizant of your own theological approach, you can bring it into dialogue with other approaches and can be critical of them as well as of your own orientation.

FOUR CONTEMPORARY THEOLOGICAL FAMILIES[1]

Revisionary Theology

Revisionary theology with its distinctive emphasis on *preaching by means of mutual critical correlation* aims to help the preacher make a Christian witness that is intelligible and morally credible in today's setting. Revisionary theology considers two sources of authority—Christian tradition and contemporary experience. Tradition includes materials from the past (the Bible, historical phenomena, affirmations of faith, doctrines, and practices). The contemporary pole is the worldview of communities today. As the term "revisionary" implies, these theologians revise their interpretations of the world (and its potential) from the perspective of Christian tradition, and their interpretation of Christian tradition from the perspective of contemporary experience.

Mutual critical correlation is key. Revisionary theologians intend to correlate Christian tradition with the contemporary world. The correlation is mutual because it assumes that the past and present can inform each other. The correlation is critical because the tradition criticizes present ways of thinking and acting, while, at the same time, the preacher critiques aspects of the tradition from the perspective of contemporary insight. Revisionary preaching sets up a conversation that moves toward mutual, critical correlation between Christian tradition and the contemporary setting.

Revisionary theology has potential weaknesses. It can be so captivated by the Zeitgeist that it revises Christian tradition only to make that tradition acceptable to contemporary ideas and mores. The distinctiveness of Christian witness can

TABLE 1. Relating Contemporary and Historic Theological Families

	Revisionary	Postliberal	Liberation	Evangelical
Orthodox				
Roman Catholic				
Anglican, Episcopalian				
Lutheran				
Reformed	Ron Allen			
Wesleyan				
Anabaptist				
Pentecostal				
Other churches descended from radical reformation				
Society of Friends				
Community and Bible churches				

disappear. Preachers sometimes mindlessly revise Christian tradition on the basis of nothing more than the latest whims of pop culture, or their own feelings. This approach can be unsettling to congregations as they puzzle over which Christian affirmations are enduring and which will be the next to be revised.

Postliberal Theology

Postliberals think that the church should interpret Christian existence (and the world) from the standpoint of Christian narratives, assumptions, doctrines, and practices. They object to the church allowing its testimony to be critiqued by standards outside the Christian house and especially object to evaluating the Bible and other dimensions of Christian life against criteria from the modern (Enlightenment) worldview. As the term "postliberal" suggests, these theologians are dissatisfied with the liberal spirit of the modern world and its scientific and experiential standards for determining truth. Postliberal theologians maintain that the Christian vision of the world, particularly in its biblical formulation, is the norm for the church. Christian community should allow scripture and orthodox Christian materials to describe the world. The church "is not to make the gospel credible to the modern world, but to make the world credible to the gospel."[2]

The church can interpret scripture as it does any good story by recognizing that some elements in the narrative are not factually correct, even while recognizing that the overall portrayal of the world in the narrative is trustworthy in its interpretation of the purpose of life and the divine character and intention. The preacher should not try to establish the credibility of Christian theology on the basis of the degree to which it satisfies modern standards for truth. Instead, the Christian community should learn the vocabulary of Christian theology (especially from the Bible). The church can then learn to describe the world from the perspective of normative Christian vision.

A major intention of postliberal preaching, then, is to lead the church to interpret the world as it is described in scripture and other orthodox Christian materials and perspectives. The sermon seeks less to help the community make sense of Christian tradition than to help the congregation understand how the tradition makes sense of the contemporary world. The preacher narrates the congregation into the story of scripture.

Postliberal theologians urge the church to maintain its distinctive identity even in the face of contemporary challenges. However, postliberalism has certain weaknesses. We cannot speak casually of *the* Christian story. As we saw in chapter 2, Christian traditions are not univocal but multivocal. The postliberal preacher must face the question, "Which version of the Christian narrative do I follow?" Postliberals are also vexed by the issue of truth. A congregation needs to know those things on which it can count in the everyday world, and those things on which it cannot count. By sidestepping the criteria for truthfulness, the congregation is left without adequate standards to identify Christian claims on which it can count. Furthermore, in my view, postliberal reasoning is circular: the preacher seeks for a community to consent to the vision of life in scripture because that vision is the one to which the community subscribes. Not surprisingly, postliberal preachers sometimes struggle with biblical texts and elements of Christian tradition that are theologically or morally problematic.

Liberation Theology

Liberation theologians believe that God intends to liberate the world from all forms of oppression. For this theology, oppression is a mode of sin in which individuals or groups repress other individuals and groups (as well as nature). Oppressors profit socially or economically by repression. Repressive forces are seldom the outcome of individual human actions but more often are systemic, that is, they are woven into patterns of thought and behavior that are constitutive of a whole social world. The following are among the most obvious forms of oppression: racism, sexism, poverty, classism, ageism, handicappism, and violation of the environment. Christian faith (and other religions) can be repressive, as well. Liberation theologians reflect from the perspective of the particular communities in which they are involved. African American women, for instance, develop African American womanist theologies. Latin American women develop mujerista theologies.

Liberation theologians see God at work in historical events to liberate the world from oppression and to bring about relationships of love, justice, mutual respect, and freedom. The best liberation theologians perceive that the act of oppression is itself oppressive and, therefore, that oppressors need to be liberated from their involvement in oppression. Liberation theology announces a renewed social world that God is bringing about in cooperation with oppressed peoples who are rising up to claim their liberation. Some liberation theologians also cooperate with oppressors who repent of repression and join the movement toward a society of shared goods and power.

The liberation preacher encourages the church to name oppression. The sermon takes another step to help the church name particular people and events through which liberation is taking place today. The preacher guides the community in responding to God's initiatives for liberation, and helps the congregation recognize what it needs to do to join God in the struggle for liberation.

A potential difficulty of liberation theology is that it can caricature both oppressor and oppressed, particularly by portraying the oppressed as altogether innocent and good and oppressors as altogether evil. In point of fact, communities that are repressed are blends of good and bad. The same is true of persons and communities who engage in repression. Liberation preaching needs to respect the complexity of persons, groups, and situations and avoid focusing so heavily on material, social, and political dimensions of liberation that it bypasses other dimensions of human existence.

Evangelical Theology

Although the evangelical theological world is pluralistic, evangelical theologians share several important perspectives. They typically believe that God inspired the Bible, although the evangelical community contains multiple notions of inspiration. Scripture, of course, is the most important source of the human perception of God. Most evangelical preachers think of scripture as a document of self-consistent revelation whose authority is universally valid. Many evangelical preachers regard scripture and Christian orthodoxy as theologically continuous. Many preachers in this domain subscribe to the understanding of truth as the correspondence of claim and reality. Scripture is truthful because its claims correspond with reality.

Evangelicals recognize that the church must explain scripture and its meaning. Thoughtful evangelicals recognize, further, that the human interpreters of the Bible can make mistakes. This recognition is why the evangelical theological world is divided into so many camps. The evangelical sermon aims, in part, to explain the Bible so that the community can understand it correctly and then apply its truth to their world.

A generation ago, evangelical preaching was mainly propositional. The preacher assumed that each biblical passage contains truthful propositions. The preacher stated the propositions clearly, presented them to the congregation, and drew out the implications. Of late, many evangelical preachers recognize that revelation can be expressed in forms other than propositions. Consequently, evangelical preaching is itself more diverse in form, though evangelical content remains the norm.

Evangelical preaching aims to be thoroughgoing in Christian perspective. Evangelical preachers are passionate, and their passion is fueled by painstaking research, especially with the biblical languages. The teaching quality that is central in many evangelical messages is a welcome emphasis in a contemporary congregation whose theology is undersized.

However, evangelical theology has soft spots. These theologians sometimes overlook the diversity that seems so evident in scripture and Christian tradition. Evangelical preachers are also often reluctant to acknowledge theological, intellectual, or moral difficulties with a text.

ELEVEN HISTORIC CHRISTIAN MOVEMENTS[3]

Preaching in churches and Christian communities should relate the gospel of the God of Israel to the congregation and world in which the sermon comes to life. However, different movements in Christian history have developed their own characteristic approaches to preaching, which are distinctive in theological content and homiletical purpose. At the risk of oversimplification, I now briefly describe leading characteristics in the preaching of eleven Christian communities.[4]

The *Orthodox* Church views the entire service of worship as sacramental. The sacrament of the word is made up of scripture readings and the sermon. The Orthodox sermon is much more than an explanation of scripture and doctrine. This sermon is similar to a verbal icon. For the Orthodox, an icon represents essential theological insight. As the worshiping community contemplates the icon, it experiences the theological reality expressed by the icon. The sermon is thus a medium through which theological reality is rendered into present experience. By participating in the sermon, the congregation participates in the theological reality spoken in the sermon. The Holy Spirit powers this iconic quality. The Orthodox tradition places very little emphasis on personal creativity in preaching. Pastors see themselves as pipelines through which the historic gospel comes alive for the community.

Roman Catholic preaching today is indebted to the Second Vatican Council (1963–65). Before Vatican II, priests and other preachers usually thought of the sermon as an explanation of doctrine. The preacher did not always relate the sermon to scripture or to other aspects of the service. By contrast, the Second Vatican Council called for four emphases in preaching:[5] (1) The sermon is to be based on the Bible, while taking account of ecclesial doctrine. (2) The sermon is to be integrated into the Christian year and is typically to be based on a passage from the official lectionary of the church. (3) The theological content of the sermon is indicative rather than imperative, that is, the proclamation is to center on the good news of what God is doing for the world and not merely on moral instruction. (4) Preaching is to take place in language and style that are familiar to the people. Preachers are encouraged to use personal stories and perceptions (including their fears and doubts) as lenses through which to focus the gospel for the congregation. Preaching is not officially a sacrament in the Roman Catholic Church, though it interprets the sacraments and can mediate grace.

Not surprisingly, preaching in the *Anglican* and *Episcopalian* churches is similar to that of the Roman Catholic Church. The sermon in the Anglican communion is based on the biblical passage, responsive to its liturgical context (usually eucharistic), kerygmatic, and adapted to the language of the local community. The scripture passages for the sermon are taken from a lectionary. The task of the preacher is to help the congregation discern how the passages from the Bible help interpret the world of the congregation in view of the themes of the Christian year and Christian doctrine. Preaching in this tradition is sacramental in the sense that the Spirit manifests the Real Presence of Christ through the words of the sermon. The pastor seeks to help the congregation name how the readings from scripture and the themes of the Christian year help them encounter the Real Presence. Along the way, sermons also help the congregation interpret the liturgy itself, as well as wider aspects of church doctrine and witness.

In a similar vein, preaching among *Lutherans* focuses on the Bible as presented through a lectionary, and takes account of the contexts of the Christian year and its place in the service of worship. Much Lutheran preaching contains the elements of law and gospel. From Luther's perspective, the law demonstrates human sin and the inability of human beings to save ourselves. However, the gospel is that God justifies us by grace. Lutheran sermons are to lead the congregation into the knowledge of God's grace revealed through Jesus Christ. The sermon sometimes guides the community in how to respond to that grace. Luther stresses that *God* speaks through the words of the preacher to make the members of the congregation aware of their helpless state and, more, to assure them that God graciously does for them what they cannot do. Preaching is also a battlefield in which God confronts Satan and the demonic powers that oppress human beings. The Lutheran preacher exposes justification by works as one of the most heinous possibilities to entrap the human being.

Preaching in the *Reformed tradition* is virtually synonymous with teaching. Following the direction of Calvin, Reformed sermons are clear and direct. The sermon names divine grace in a passage from the Bible and shows how that grace continues to work in the world and particularly how it calls forth faith. Whereas Luther saw the law as almost altogether negative, Calvin posited a third use of the law that has an implication for preaching: just as the law provides guidance for life, so the sermon leads the congregation in discerning how to live faithfully in response to God's electing grace. For many years, Reformed pastors often preached in the pattern of *lectio continua*—preaching continuously from whole books of the Bible. The Reformed tradition in preaching is found today in the various Presbyterian bodies, the Reformed Church, parts of the United Church of Christ, and in the Christian Church (Disciples of Christ), the Christian Churches affiliated with the North American Christian Convention, and the Churches of Christ.

Wesleyan sermons seek to speak "plain truth for plain people."[6] In Wesley's day, much preaching in the established churches had become quite ornate. Wesley found the flourishes of such preaching distracting, and called for simple explanation of the gospel in such a way that the Spirit could work in the hearts of the listeners. Preachers in this tradition aim to help the congregation members become aware of their need for God. Christ is an expression of God's love for them. The sermon is designed to lead the community in the path of sanctification, that is, in growth in the ways of God for personal and social life. In Wesleyan perspective, the Holy Spirit is ever trying to create a climate of receptivity toward God's grace in human beings; however, people have the choice of embracing or denying this grace. The Spirit is also always prompting the self and the community toward holiness (living in ways that testify to God's grace). This approach to preaching is characteristic of the African Methodist Episcopal Church, the African Methodist Episcopal Zion Church, the Christian Methodist Episcopal Church, the United Methodist Church, and other Wesleyan and Holiness communions.

Anabaptists took the Reformation emphasis on worship to a new level of simplicity. Their worship consists mainly of singing, prayers, and other parts of worship composed locally. Preaching is typically the climax of the service. In the *Baptist* congregations, the preacher intends to awaken the congregation to divine grace revealed in Jesus Christ, and invites the congregation to decide to affirm that grace and live in it. Preachers also invite the congregation to make decisions to participate in church programs, or to take stands on personal and social issues. This kind of preaching is found in many congregations in the wide-ranging Baptist spectrum: American, independent, Missionary, National, Progressive, Southern, and others.

A more disjunctive element in the relationship between church and culture is found in other *churches descended from the radical reformation*. According to these communions, the Christian community is to keep itself separated from the world for the purpose of maintaining purity of life within the congregation as well as purity of witness to the larger world. Whereas Baptist bodies often see evangelism as the ultimate goal of the sermon, these communities see the sermon as a means to growth in discipleship and witness. The Bible is a primary source of guidance. The Mennonites are leading exemplars of these patterns.

Silent aspects of worship are one of the hallmarks of the *Society of Friends*. Such worship relies on the direct movement of the Spirit in the assembly to lead members to speak. Indeed, some Friends believe that the risen Christ continues directly to teach the contemporary community by means of the Spirit speaking through members. In addition, many meetings (congregations) have a form of worship (sometimes called programmed worship) that includes a sermon. The originator of the Friends, George Fox, was a noted preacher. The sermon, in this context, not only names the grace of God and interprets the divine leading for the community, but can also be a means through which Christ teaches the congregation.

Pentecostal theologians are often evangelical in general theological orientation. Pentecostals and evangelicals differ in that Pentecostals call attention to the importance of the Spirit in the Bible, in Christian tradition, and especially for the church today. The Spirit fills the believer and the community with the ecstatic awareness of the presence of God (often manifest through speaking in tongues and other remarkable phenomena), empowers the community for witness, and sparks the community to anticipate the second coming of Jesus. Pentecostal preachers think that the Holy Spirit inspires preaching. Some pentecostal preachers have such confidence in spontaneous inspiration that they make little preparation for the sermon other than to pray. They do not want the human will to get in the way of the words and experience the Spirit seeks to bring about in worship. Most preachers in this family, however, think that the Spirit can anoint the pastor in the process of preparing the sermon as well as when the preacher steps to the pulpit. In a similar way, the Holy Spirit leads the community toward receptivity. Of course, the pentecostal sermon announces the grace of God through Christ, while going ahead to emphasize the immediate presence and leading of the Spirit. The preacher also stresses the responsibility of the congregation members to act on the gifts of the Spirit in their midst. Pentecostal preachers meditate on ways the Spirit directs them in interpreting a Bible passage, while also meditating on ways that the text helps the congregation recognize the presence and leading of the Spirit.

The *community churches* and the *Bible churches* (and congregations that are known similarly) are increasing in number in North America. While they do not have a crisp historical identity (as do, say, the Lutheran churches), they share an evangelical orientation to theology. Like many churches of the past, they seek to return to a simple form of biblical Christianity that is free of ecclesiastical overlay and theological tribalism. Since the divinely inspired Bible is the primary source of faith and practice, the raison d'être of the sermon is explaining the Bible and applying it to life.

Such brief sketches cannot do justice to the richness and complexity of individual traditions of preaching or track developments that have taken place within the histories of these traditions. Nor can this list enumerate the full range of preaching communities, especially the hybrids that emerge. However, even a cursory summary helps preachers name and value the qualities of preaching characteristic of their community, and to reflect theologically on the adequacy of that tradition.

Bibliography of Helps for Preaching Doctrine and Systematic Theology

This short bibliography lists and very briefly annotates some works that discuss the relationship among preaching, doctrine, and systematic theology. The bibliography deals only with the current period and is representative, not exhaustive.

Allen, Ronald J. *Interpreting the Gospel: An Introduction to Preaching*. St. Louis: Chalice Press, 1998. Twenty-seven-step guide to sermons on biblical texts, Christian doctrines, Christian practices, and topics.

———. *Preaching the Topical Sermon*. Louisville, Ky.: Westminster/John Knox Press, 1992. Develops notion of preaching theology under rubric of topical preaching. Contains bibliography of older works on doctrinal preaching.

———. "Two Approaches to Theology and Their Implications for Preaching," *Journal for Preachers* 19/3 (1995), 38–48. Compares and contrasts revisionary and postliberal approaches to preaching.

Bond, L. Susan. *Trouble with Jesus: Women, Christology, and Preaching*. St. Louis: Chalice Press, 1999. Theological analysis of Christology for preaching from points of view of women's theologies.

Brouwer, Wayne. "Preaching the Heidelberg Catechism," *Reformed Worship* 26 (1992), 38–39. Three strategies for developing sermons on the Heidelberg Catechism, which can be adapted to preaching other bodies of doctrine.

Brown, R. E. C. "The Exposition of Doctrine," in his *The Ministry of the Word*. 1958. Reprint, Philadelphia: Fortress Press, 1976, 41–51. Concentrates on the importance of the process of thinking doctrinally in preaching rather than on content of doctrine.

Buttrick, David G. *A Captive Voice: The Liberation of Preaching*. Louisville, Ky.: Westminster John Knox Press, 1994. Calls for "turn to theology" in preaching.

———. *Homiletic: Moves and Structures*. Philadelphia: Fortress Press, 1987. His "preaching in reflective mode" and especially "preaching as praxis" articulate practical ways of engaging in systematic theological reflection.

Carl, William J., III. *Preaching Christian Doctrine*. Philadelphia: Fortress Press, 1983. Doctrine in relationship to Bible, Christian year, and culture.

Ellingsen, Mark. "Doctrine," in *Concise Encyclopedia for Preaching*, ed. William Willimon and Richard Lischer. Louisville, Ky.: Westminster John Knox Press, 1995, 104. Doctrinal catechesis necessary in preaching to develop identity of church.

———. *Doctrine and Word: Theology in the Pulpit*. Atlanta: John Knox Press, 1983. Mini-systematic theology with notes on preaching and sample sermons.

Erickson, Millard J., and James L. Heflin. *New Wine in Old Wineskins: Doctrinal Preaching in a Changing World*. Grand Rapids: Baker Book House, 1997. Relationship of exposition and doctrine from evangelical perspective.

Farley, Edward. "Preaching the Bible and Preaching the Gospel," *Theology Today* 51 (1994), 90–103. Stresses preaching the gospel taking priority over preaching the Bible.

Faulkener, Joseph. "What Are They Saying? A Content Analysis of 206 Sermons Preached in the Christian Church (Disciples of Christ) during 1988," in *A Case Study of Mainstream Protestantism: The Disciples' Relation to American Culture, 1880–1990*, ed. D. Newell Williams. Grand Rapids: Wm. B. Eerdmans Publishing Co., and St. Louis: Chalice Press, 1991. Finds that doctrine in today's sermons is more "declamation than analytical explanation," abstract.

Forde, Gerhard. *Theology Is for Proclamation*. Fortress Resources for Preaching. Minneapolis: Fortress Press, 1990. Theology clarifies content of proclamation.

George, Timothy. "Doctrinal Preaching," in *Handbook of Contemporary Preaching*, ed. Michael Duiduit. Nashville: Broadman Press, 1992, 93. Regards recovery of doctrine in preaching as essential to renewal of church.

Hall, Thor. *The Future Shape of Preaching*. Philadelphia: Fortress Press, 1971. Preaching gives voice to theology.

Hilkert, Mary Catherine. *Naming Grace: Preaching and the Sacramental Imagination*. New York: Continuum Publishing Co., 1997. In the midst of developing a theology of preaching, Hilkert reflects on theological content of the sermon.

———. "Preaching and Theology," *Worship* 65 (1991), 398–409. Preacher as theologian.

Hill, William J. "Preaching as a 'Moment' in Theology," *Homiletic and Pastoral Review* 77 (1976), 10–19. Relationship of experience and theology in preaching.

Hinkle, Mary A. "American Protestant Preaching: A Twentieth Century Perspective," *Word and World* 20 (2000), 96–109. Preaching as constructive theology.

Hughes, Robert, and Robert Kysar, *Preaching Doctrine for the Twenty-First Century*. Minneapolis: Fortress Press, 1997. "Homiletic theology" for postmodernity with attention to "moments of theological reflection" and theology in images and story.

Kemper, Robert G. "How Preaching Creates Theology," *Christian Ministry* 28 (1997), 13–14. Ways in which preaching calls forth theological reflection and discovery.

Lischer, Richard. *A Theology of Preaching: Dynamics of the Gospel*, rev. ed. Durham, N.C.: Labrynth Press, 1992. In midst of profound attention to theology of preaching, stresses importance of theological content in sermons.

———. "The Interrupted Sermon," *Interpretation* 59 (1996), 169–80. Renewal of preaching begins with the recovery of the church's distinctive theological language.

———. "Preaching as the Church's Language," in *Listening to the Word: Studies in Honor of Fred B. Craddock*, ed. Gail R. O'Day and Thomas G. Long. Nashville: Abingdon Press, 1993, 113–30. Preaching as theological language has the power to form Christian community.

———. "Preaching as Theology," in *Preaching and Worship*. Papers of the 1980 Meeting of the Academy of Homiletics, ed. Leroy Kennel, 52–61. Preaching is final expression, and norm, of theology.

Long, Thomas G., and Edward Farley, eds. *Preaching as a Theological Task: World, Gospel, Scripture*. In Honor of David Buttrick. Louisville, Ky.: Westminster John Knox Press, 1996. Sixteen essays on aspects of theology and preaching.

Lueking, F. Dean. "The Pastor as Theologian," *Christian Ministry* 30/6 (1999), 6–81. Respected pastor meditates on the relationship between pastoral work and theology.

Massey, James Earl. *Designing the Sermon*. Abingdon Preacher's Guides. Nashville: Abingdon Press, 1980, 35–49. Classic discussion of doctrinal preaching.

McClure, John S. "Changes in Authority, Method, and Message in Presbyterian (UPCUSA) Preaching in the Twentieth Century," in *The Confessional Mosaic: Presbyterians and Twentieth Century Theology*, ed. Milton J. Coalter, John M. Mulder, and Louis B. Weeks. Louisville, Ky.: Westminster/John Knox Press, 1990. Traces decline of theological clarity in preaching. Focuses on Presbyterianism, but observations apply to other long-established denominations.

———, and Burton Cooper, "Preaching and the Question of Reformed Theology," *Journal for Preachers* 16 (1992), 25–30. Importance of Reformed preachers knowing reformed theology in the context of "reformed and always reforming."

———. *The Four Codes of Preaching: Rhetorical Strategies*. Philadelphia: Fortress Press, 1991. Discussion of theosymbolic code helps preachers articulate actual theology of congregation.

McKim, Donald K. *The Bible in Theology and Preaching*. 1985. Reprint, Nashville: Abingdon Press, 1994. Twelve ways of doing theology with outcomes for interpreting the Bible and preaching. Illustrative sermons.

Nestingen, James Arne. "Preaching the Catechism," *Word & World* 10 (1990), 33–42. Lutheran paradigm for preaching a catechism, especially in Christian year.

Neville, Robert Cumings. *The God Who Beckons: Theology in the Form of Ser-mons*. Nashville: Abingdon Press, 1999. Sermons with explicit atten-tion to systematic theology.

Plantinga, Cornelius Jr. "Preaching Sin to Reluctant Hearers," *Perspectives* 12 (1997), 8–12. Strategies for preaching on the doctrine of sin. Principles apply also to other doctrines.

Reymond, Bernard. "Homiletics and Theology: Re-evaluating Their Rela-tionship," *Modern Churchman* 34 (1993), 29–43. Invites theology to place itself under the guidance of preaching.

Smith, Christine M. *Preaching as Weeping, Confession, and Resistance: Radical Responses to Radical Evil*. Louisville, Ky.: Westminster/John Knox Press, 1992. Penetrating theological deconstruction of forms of systemic evil for preaching.

———, ed. *Preaching Justice: Ethnic and Cultural Perspectives*. Cleveland: United Church Press, 1998. Essays analyze the relationship between theology, culture, and preaching in eight different communities.

Stricklen, Teresa Lockhart. "The Relationship of Preaching and Theology: Introduction to a Work in Progress," *The Academy of Homiletics: Papers of the Annual Meeting* (1998), 1–13. Overview of author's Ph.D. disser-tation at Vanderbilt University that critiques current understandings of the interplay of theology and preaching and poses a constructive alter-native in view of the work of Edward Farley.

Thompson, James W. *Preaching Like Paul: Homiletical Wisdom for Today*. Louisville, Ky.: Westminster John Knox Press, 2001, 107–26. Draws on the writings of Paul as model for theologically reflective preaching.

Tisdale, Leonora Tubbs. *Preaching as Local Theology and Folk Art*. Fortress Resources for Preaching. Minneapolis: Fortress Press, 1997. Consid-ers relationship of doctrine and local theologies.

Van Seters, Arthur. "Dilemmas in Preaching Doctrine: Declaricalizing Proclamation," *Journal for Preachers* 17/3 (1994). Shows how doctrine can be a direct help to the preacher.

Wallace, Catherine M. "Storytelling, Doctrine, and Spiritual Formation," *Anglican Theological Review* 81 (1999), 39–59. Relationship between story and doctrine.

Warren, Timothy S. "The Theological Process in Sermon Preparation," *Bib-liotheca Sacra* 156 (1999), 336–56. Practical steps for integrating theo-logical consciousness into all phases of preparing the sermon.

Webb, Joseph M. *Preaching and the Challenge of Pluralism*. St. Louis: Chalice Press, 1998. Symbolic interactionism as clue to uses of theological symbols.

Wilson, Frank T. "Doctrinal Preaching," *Journal of the Interdenominational Theological Center* 9 (1982), 121–26. Calls preachers to "This I Believe" sermons.

Wilson, Paul Scott. "Doctrine in Preaching: Has It a Future?" in *Preaching on the Brink*, ed. Martha J. Simmons. Nashville: Abingdon Press, 1996, 84–91. Sees heightened role for doctrine in preaching in future.

————. *The Four Pages of the Sermon: A Guide to Biblical Preaching*. Nashville: Abingdon Press, 1999. Urges preacher to concentrate on one doctrine in each sermon.

————. *Imagination of the Heart: New Understandings in Preaching*. Nashville: Abingdon Press, 1988. Lucid analysis of relationship among doctrine, image, and story.

————. *The Practice of Preaching*. Nashville: Abingdon Press, 1995. Invites preachers to integrate doctrine into process of preparing and preaching sermons.

Notes

Introduction

1. David Buttrick, *A Captive Voice: The Liberation of Preaching* (Louisville, Ky.: Westminster John Knox Press, 1994), 110–12; Edward Farley, "Preaching the Bible and Preaching the Gospel," *Theology Today* 51 (1994), 90–103; idem. "Toward a New Paradigm for Preaching," *Preaching as a Theological Task: World, Gospel, Scripture. In Honor of David Buttrick,* ed. Thomas G. Long and Edward Farley (Louisville, Ky.: Westminster John Knox Press, 1996), 176–88.

Chapter 1: Systematic Theology as a Pastoral Resource

1. For a readable explanation of theology and basic current bibliography, see Donald G. Luck, *Why Study Theology* (St. Louis: Chalice Press, 1999).
2. On the relationship between systematic theology and homiletic theology, see Robert G. Hughes and Robert Kysar, *Preaching Doctrine for the Twenty-First Century.* Fortress Resources for Preaching (Minneapolis: Fortress Press, 1997), 25–35. I do not take up the relationship between systematic and liturgical theology. For an overview of basic literature, see Frank C. Senn, "Worship, Doctrine, and Life: Liturgical Theology, Theologies of Worship, and Doxological Theology," *Currents in Theology and Mission* 9 (1982), 11–21. For current liturgical theologies see Don E. Saliers, *Worship as Theology: Foretaste of Glory Divine* (Nashville: Abingdon Press, 1995) and Gordon Lathrop, *Holy Things: A Liturgical Theology* (Minneapolis: Fortress Press, 1993).
3. Ellen T. Charry, *By the Renewing of Your Minds: The Pastoral Function of Christian Doctrine* (New York: Oxford University Press, 1997), 1–2. Charry explores how doctrine functioned to "form and re-form character" in representative theologians from the time of the Second Testament to the seventeenth century.
4. David Ford gives an overview of many recent theologians and theological movements in his *The Modern Theologians: An Introduction to Christian Theology in the Twentieth Century.* 2d ed. (Cambridge: Blackwell, 1997).

5. Alister E. McGrath, *The Genesis of Doctrine: A Study in the Foundations of Doctrinal Criticism* (Oxford: Basil Blackwell, 1990), vii.
6. On the emergence of doctrine in relationship to specific circumstances, see Jaroslav Pelikan, *The Christian Tradition: A History of the Development of Doctrine* (New Haven, Conn.: Yale University Press, 1971–1989), 5 vols.
7. Clark M. Williamson, *Way of Blessing, Way of Life: A Christian Theology* (St. Louis: Chalice Press, 1999), 24–29.
8. Ibid., 29–32. These criteria are adapted for preaching in Ronald J. Allen, *Interpreting the Gospel: An Introduction to Preaching* (St. Louis: Chalice Press, 1998), 144–45.
9. Ibid., 25.

Chapter 2: Why the Church Needs Systematic Theology in Preaching Today

1. Christopher L. Morse, *Not Every Spirit: A Logic of Christian Disbelief* (Valley Forge, Pa.: Trinity Press International, 1994), passim.
2. For orientation to Christian practice, see *Practicing Our Faith: A Way of Life for a Searching People*, ed. Dorothy C. Bass (San Francisco: Jossey-Bass, 1997). On preaching and Christian practice see Ronald J. Allen, *Preaching and Practical Ministry*. Preaching and Its Partners (St. Louis: Chalice Press, 2001).
3. Craig Dykstra and Dorothy C. Bass, "Times of Yearning, Practices of Faith," in *Practicing Our Faith*, 9.
4. Representative is Robert Wuthnow, *The Restructuring of American Religion: Society and Faith since World War II* (Princeton, N.J.: Princeton University Press, 1988).
5. Wade Clark Roof and William McKinney, *American Mainline Religion* (New Brunswick, N.J.: Rutgers University Press, 1987), 164–70.
6. For the relationship between church and culture, see Clark M. Williamson and Ronald J. Allen, *The Vital Church: Teaching, Worship, Community, Service* (St. Louis: Chalice Press, 1998), 34–40.
7. Clifford Geertz, *The Interpretation of Cultures: Selected Essays* (New York: Basic Books, 1973), 90.
8. For an extended comparison between modern and postmodern worldviews, see Ronald J. Allen, Barbara Shires Blaisdell, and Scott Black Johnston, *Theology for Preaching: Authority, Truth, and Knowledge of God in a Postmodern Ethos* (Nashville: Abingdon Press, 1997), passim.
9. On postmodernism and preaching, see in addition to Allen, Blaisdell, and Johnston, *Theology for Preaching*: Robert G. Hughes and Robert Kysar, *Preaching Doctrine for the Twenty-First Century*. Fortress Resources for Preaching (Minneapolis: Fortress Press, 1997), 8–19; Joseph M. Webb, *Preaching and the Challenge of Pluralism* (St. Louis: Chalice Press, 1998); and Ronald J. Allen, "Preaching and Postmodernism," *Interpretation* 55 (2001), 34–48.
10. Hughes and Kysar probe this phenomenon in *Preaching Doctrine*, 2–6.
11. John S. McClure, "Changes in the Authority, Method, and Message

in the Presbyterian Church (UPCUSA) Preaching in the Twentieth Century," in *The Confessional Mosaic: Presbyterians and Twentieth Century Theology*, ed. Milton J. Coalter, John M. Mulder, and Louis B. Weeks (Louisville, Ky.: Westminster/John Knox Press, 1990), 108, 180 (n. 96).

12. Marsha G. Witten, *All Is Forgiven: The Secular Message in American Protestantism* (Princeton, N.J.: Princeton University Press, 1993), 18, 53.

13. Joseph E. Faulkener, "What Are They Saying? A Content Analysis of 206 Sermons Preached in the Christian Church (Disciples of Christ) During 1988," in *A Case Study of Mainstream Protestantism*, ed. D. Newell Williams (Grand Rapids: Wm. B. Eerdmans Publishing Co., and St. Louis: Chalice Press, 1991), 416.

14. David Buttrick, *A Captive Voice: The Liberation of Preaching* (Louisville, Ky.: Westminster John Knox Press, 1994), 112.

15. Emmanuel Levinas, *Otherwise than Being or Beyond Essence*, tr. Alphonso Lingis (1974; reprint, Pittsburgh: Duquesne University Press, 1981), 49, 189.

16. Emmanuel Levinas, *Totality and Infinity*, tr. Alphonso Lingis (1961; reprint, Pittsburgh: University of Duquesne Press, 1969), 43–44.

17. On preaching and otherness, see Webb, *The Challenge of Pluralism*, 112–18; Allen, "Preaching and Postmodernism," 40–42; idem., "Preaching and the Other," *Worship* (forthcoming).

18. Lyle Schaller, "How Long Is the Sermon?" *The Parish Paper* 1, no. 11 (1994), 1.

Chapter 3: Biblical Preaching through the Lens of Systematic Theology

1. For criticism of the practice of preaching from individual passages, see the materials from David Buttrick and Edward Farley cited in the Introduction, n. 1. For a sympathetic rejoinder, see my "Why Preach from Passages in the Bible?" in *Preaching as a Theological Task: World, Gospel, Scripture. In Honor of David Buttrick*, ed. Thomas G. Long and Edward Farley (Louisville, Ky.: Westminster John Knox Press, 1996), 176–87.

2. On the importance of preaching from the Bible, see Allen, "Why Preach from Passages in the Bible?" and idem, *Interpreting the Gospel: An Introduction to Preaching* (St. Louis: Chalice Press, 1998), 99–113.

3. See further the materials cited in the Introduction, n. 1. For other approaches, many weighted toward postliberalism, see *The Theological Interpretation of Scripture: Classic and Contemporary*, ed. Stephen E. Fowl, Blackwell Readings in Modern Theology (London: Blackwell Publishers, 1997). For a sustained attempt to read the First Testament in a theological way, see Bruce C. Birch, Walter Brueggemann, Terence E. Fretheim, and David L. Petersen, *A Theological Introduction to the Old Testament* (Nashville: Abingdon Press, 1999).

4. The insight that the Bible is theologically diverse is commonplace today. For representative theological assessments, see Paul D. Hanson,

The Diversity of Scripture, Overtures to Biblical Theology (Philadelphia: Fortress Press, 1982); John Goldingay, *Theological Diversity and the Authority of the Old Testament* (Grand Rapids: Wm. B. Eerdmans Publishing Co., 1987); James D. G. Dunn, *The Unity and Diversity of the New Testament*. 2d ed. (Philadelphia: Trinity Press International, 1990); John Reumann, *Variety and Unity in New Testament Thought* (Oxford: Oxford University Press, 1991); David Rhoads, *The Challenge of Diversity: The Witness of Paul and the Gospels* (Minneapolis: Fortress Press, 1996).

5. Ronald J. Allen and John C. Holbert, *Holy Root, Holy Branches: Christian Preaching from the Old Testament* (Nashville: Abingdon Press, 1995), 32–62.

6. Occasional systematic theologians use the Bible in much the same way, that is, as a box of propositions that they can cut out and paste into a volume of systematic theology without regard for historical or literary context.

7. For materials that bring theological concerns explicitly to the surface, see the Bibliography.

8. The journal *Lectionary Homiletics* regularly includes a section on theological reflection on passages from the Revised Common Lectionary.

9. For incisive criticism of lone-ranger approaches to the Bible, see Justo González and Catherine G. Gunzález, *The Liberating Pulpit* (Nashville: Abingdon Press, 1994).

10. For a provocative alternative model that gives greater priority to continuities between the Bible and doctrine, see William J. Carl III, *Preaching Christian Doctrine* (Philadelphia: Fortress Press, 1984), 33–57.

11. For sustained considerations of this motif, see Clark M. Williamson and Ronald J. Allen, *Adventures of the Spirit: A Guide to Worship from the Perspective of Process Theology* (Lanham, Md.: University Press of America, 1997), 114–35; William E. Dorman and Ronald J. Allen, "Preaching as Hospitality," *Quarterly Review* 14 (1994), 295–310, as well as Ronald J. Allen, "Preaching and the Other," *Worship* (forthcoming); and Fernando F. Segovia, "The Text as Other: Towards a Hispanic American Hermeneutic," in *Text and Experience: Towards a Cultural Exegesis of the Bible*, ed. Daniel Smith-Christopher (Sheffield: Sheffield Academic Press, 1995), 276–99.

12. Cf. Carol Schersten LaHurd, "The 'Other' in Biblical Perspective," *Currents in Theology and Mission* 24 (1997), 411–29.

13. Edward Farley, *Good and Evil: Interpreting a Human Condition* (Minneapolis: Fortress Press, 1990), 35.

14. Mark Kline Taylor, *Remembering Esperanza: A Cultural-Political Theology for North American Praxis* (Maryknoll, N.Y.: Orbis Books, 1990), 61.

15. David Tracy, *Plurality and Ambiguity: Hermeneutics, Religion, Hope* (San Francisco: Harper and Row, 1987), 15.

16. Ibid., 20.

17. Robert G. Hughes and Robert Kysar offer an excellent exegetical approach to identifying the theology of a particular passage within the larger theology of the book in which the text is found in their *Preaching Doctrine for the Twenty-First Century*. Fortress Resources for Preaching (Minneapolis: Fortress Press, 1997), 36–53.

18. For representative summaries of methods in contemporary biblical scholarship, see David L. Bartlett, *Between the Bible and the Church: New Methods for Biblical Preaching* (Nashville: Abingdon Press, 1999); *To Each Its Own Meaning: An Introduction to Biblical Criticisms and Their Application*, ed. Steven L. McKenzie and Stephen L. Haynes (Louisville, Ky.: Westminster John Knox Press, 1999); Stephen Farris, *Preaching That Matters: The Bible and Our Lives* (Louisville, Ky.: Westminster John Knox Press, 1998); Ronald J. Allen, *Contemporary Biblical Interpretation for Preaching* (Valley Forge, Pa.: Judson Press, 1984).

19. For an earlier form of such questions, see Clark M. Williamson and Ronald J. Allen, *A Credible and Timely Word: Process Theology and Preaching* (St. Louis: Chalice Press, 1991), 93–101.

20. Paul Scott Wilson, *Imagination of the Heart: New Understandings in Preaching* (Nashville: Abingdon Press, 1988), 166–69.

21. For fuller statements of surface and depth dimensions in texts, see Williamson and Allen, *A Credible and Timely Word*, 96–101; Allen, *Interpreting the Gospel*, 88–91.

22. William C. Placher, *Unapologetic Theology: A Christian Voice in a Pluralistic Conversation* (Louisville, Ky.: Westminster/John Knox Press, 1989), 130.

23. For an earlier version of these questions, see Williamson and Allen, *A Credible and Timely Word*, 101–11.

24. Robert G. Hughes and Robert Kysar recommend that sermons contain moments of direct theological reflection, moments of theological learning, of speaking the gospel directly, of questioning, of organizing scattered thoughts in their *Preaching Doctrine*, 74–93.

25. Arthur Van Seters, "Dilemmas of Preaching Doctrine: Declericalizing Proclamation," *Journal for Preachers* 17, no. 3 (1994), 34.

Chapter 4: The Sermon in the Form of Systematic Theology

1. On differences between doctrine and systematic theology, see pp. 12–15.

2. From the standpoint of traditional classifications of sermon, this chapter advocates a topical approach to preaching. See Ronald J. Allen, *Preaching the Topical Sermon* (Louisville, Ky.: Westminster/John Knox Press, 1992) and William J. Carl III, *Preaching Christian Doctrine* (Philadelphia: Fortress Press, 1984).

3. Carl, *Preaching Christian Doctrine*, 34–35.

4. The expository sermon often contains a lot of material that directly explains the text in its various contexts (sociohistorical, literary, theological). However, a sermon cannot be considered expository strictly

on the basis of the amount of overt discussion of the Bible in the sermon. Some expository sermons devote little time to biblical exegesis as such, but interpret the text by other means, e.g., images, stories, poems, reflections.

5. Marjorie Hewitt Suchocki, *God, Christ, Church: A Practical Guide to Process Theology*, rev. ed. (New York: Crossroad Publishing Co., 1989), 14–15.

6. For a summary of historic affirmations in Christian tradition, see Ted A. Campbell, *Christian Confessions: A Historical Introduction* (Louisville, Ky.: Westminster John Knox Press, 1996); cf. John Leith, *Creeds of the Churches: A Reader in Christian Doctrine from the Bible to the Present*, rev. ed. (Richmond: John Knox Press, 1973).

7. For more fully developed methodologies, see Carl, *Preaching Christian Doctrine*, 59–95; Allen, *Preaching the Topical Sermon*, 37–71; idem, *Interpreting the Gospel*, 97–176.

8. The preacher might adapt the approach to making an analogy between the biblical and contemporary worlds developed by Stephen Farris, *Preaching That Matters: The Bible and Our Lives* (Louisville, Ky.: Westminster John Knox Press, 1998) to making an analogy between the world that gives rise to an affirmation of doctrine or theology and today's world.

9. Clark M. Williamson, *Way of Blessing, Way of Life* (St. Louis: Chalice Press, 1999), 119–20.

10. Ibid., 118.

11. Women's theological movements are immensely pluralistic—embracing a wide range of persons of European, African, Latina, Asian, and Native American origin. Many racial and ethnic women resist the designation *feminist* because of its close association with European American women. A number of males are sympathetic to feminist themes.

12. Of course, women interpret the very notion of "experience" in many ways. Mary Catherine Hilkert summarizes in her "Experience and Tradition—Can the Center Hold? Revelation" in *Freeing Theology: The Essentials of Theology in Feminist Perspective*, ed. Catherine Mowry LaCugna (San Francisco: HarperSanFrancisco, 1993), 76–77.

13. L. Susan Bond, *Trouble with Jesus: Women, Christology and Preaching* (St. Louis: Chalice Press, 1999), 39–75.

14. On the provocative motif of salvage, see ibid., 120–23.

15. Ibid., 49.

16. Ibid., 114.

17. Ibid., 115.

Chapter 5: Making Theology Lively in the Sermon

1. *Patterns for Preaching: A Sermon Sampler*, ed. Ronald J. Allen (St. Louis: Chalice Press, 1998). Robert G. Hughes and Robert Kysar have an excellent discussion of sermon form in their *Preaching Doctrine for the Twenty-First Century*, Fortress Resources for Preaching (Minneapolis: Fortress Press, 1997), 94–112.

2. Paul Scott Wilson, *The Four Pages of the Sermon* (Nashville: Abingdon Press, 1999).
3. This approach is discussed in Ronald J. Allen, *Preaching the Topical Sermon* (Louisville, Ky.: Westminster/John Knox Press, 1992), 81–84.
4. For discussion see *Patterns of Preaching*, 117–23.
5. From a sermon preached at First Christian Church (Disciples of Christ), Omaha, Nebraska.
6. This suggestion permeates Wilson's work, e.g., *The Four Pages of the Sermon*, 44–49.
7. Barbara Brown Taylor, *Speaking of Sin: The Lost Language of Salvation* (Boston: Cowley Publications, 2000), 90–91.
8. Ibid., 91–93.
9. Paul Tillich, "You Are Accepted," in his *The Shaking of the Foundations* (New York: Charles Scribner's Sons, 1948), 162.
10. Paul Tillich, *Systematic Theology: Three Volumes in One* (Chicago: University of Chicago Press, 1967), vol. 1, 59–66.
11. Ibid., 49.
12. Tillich, "You Are Accepted," 162.
13. Ibid., 162–63.
14. Marjorie Hewitt Suchocki, *The Whispered Word: A Theology of Preaching* (St. Louis: Chalice Press, 1999), 86–87.
15. Ibid., 87–89.
16. On the importance of story and image in preaching doctrine and theology, see Hughes and Kysar, *Preaching Doctrine*, 54–73, as well as Paul Scott Wilson, *Imagination of the Heart: New Understandings in Preaching* (Nashville: Abingdon Press, 1988), 143–87.
17. Charles R. Blaisdell, sermon preached at First Christian Church (Disciples of Christ), Concord, California.
18. Robert G. Hughes and Robert Kysar amplify this discussion in their *Preaching Doctrine*, 74–78, 85–89.
19. From a sermon preached at Trinity Presbyterian Church, Nashville, Tennessee.
20. One of the best discussions of questions that I have seen is Hughes and Kysar, *Preaching Doctrine*, 78–85.
21. R. Robert Cueni, *Questions of Faith for Inquiring Believers* (Lima, Ohio: CSS Publishing Co., forthcoming).
22. From a sermon preached at Christian Theological Seminary, Indianapolis, Indiana.

Chapter 6: Integrating Systematic Theology into the Preaching Calendar

1. Robert G. Hughes and Robert Kysar, *Preaching Doctrine for the Twenty-First Century*, Fortress Resources for Preaching (Minneapolis: Fortress Press, 1997), 113–22, help preachers bring a full range of doctrinal concerns in a year of preaching.
2. The most penetrating evaluation of the Revised Common Lectionary is Shelley E. Cochran, *The Pastor's Underground Guide to the Revised*

Common Lectionary (St. Louis: Chalice Press. Year A: 1995; Year B: 1996; Year C: 1997). Also very helpful is Eugene L. Lowry, *Living with the Lectionary: Preaching through the Revised Common Lectionary* (Nashville: Abingdon Press, 1992). Cf. Ronald J. Allen, *Interpreting the Gospel: An Introduction to Preaching* (St. Louis: Chalice Press, 1998), 103–9.

3. For a fuller discussion, see William J. Carl III, *Preaching Christian Doctrine* (Philadelphia: Fortress Press, 1984), 73–81.

4. On the formative power of Christian practice, see 22–25 and 150, n. 2.

5. James A. Sanders, "Canon and Calendar: An Alternative Lectionary Proposal," in *Social Themes of the Christian Year: A Commentary on the Lectionary*, ed. Dieter T. Hessel (Philadelphia: Geneva Press, 1983), 283, n. 3.

6. Cochran, *The Pastor's Underground Guide to the Revised Common Lectionary* (1995), 21.

7. Arthur Van Seters, "Dilemmas of Preaching Doctrine: Declericalizing Proclamation," *Journal for Preachers* 17, no. 3 (1994), 34.

8. Cochran, *The Pastor's Underground Guide to the Revised Common Lectionary* (1995), 25–33.

9. For example, see David Steel, *Preaching through the Year* (Atlanta: John Knox Press, 1980).

10. From a sermon preached at Westminster Presbyterian Church, Wilmington, Delaware.

11. Clark M. Williamson, *Way of Blessing, Way of Life: A Christian Theology* (St. Louis: Chalice Press, 1999).

12. Rebecca Button Prichard, *Sensing the Spirit: The Holy Spirit in Feminist Perspective* (St. Louis: Chalice Press, 1999).

13. See further, Carl, *Preaching Christian Doctrine*, 95–137.

14. R. Robert Cueni, *Questions of Faith for Inquiring Believers* (Lima, Ohio: CSS Publishing Co., forthcoming).

15. Sanders, "Canon and Calendar," 257–63.

Chapter 7: Sample Sermons

1. For the perspective on interpreting Luke–Acts that informs this sermon, see Ronald J. Allen, *Preaching Luke–Acts*, Preaching Classic Texts (St. Louis: Chalice Press, 2000).

2. The Reformers became engrossed in a fascinating debate regarding the relationship of the ascended Jesus with the Lord's Supper. While that discussion is important, it does not contribute significantly to this particular sermon. The debate is summarized with unusual succinctness in David C. Steinmetz, "Scripture and the Lord's Supper in Luther's Theology," *Interpretation* 37 (1983), 253–65.

3. Karl Barth, *Church Dogmatics: The Doctrine of Creation*, ed. G. W. Bromiley and T. F. Torrance (Edinburgh: T. & T. Clark, 1960), vol. 3, pt. 2, 453.

4. Joseph Haroutunian, "The Doctrine of the Ascension," *Interpretation* 10 (1956), 276, 278. My emphasis.

5. For some other references, see Matt. 26:64; Mark 14:62; Luke 22:69; Acts 2:33–34; 5:31; 7:55; Rom. 8:34; Eph. 1:20; Col. 3:1; Heb. 1:13; 8:1; 12:2; 1 Pet. 3:22.
6. For example, Martin Luther, "Psalm 110," in *Luther's Works*, ed. Jaroslav Pelikan (St. Louis: Concordia Publishing House, 1956), vol. 13, 233–34; John Calvin, *Commentaries on the Epistles of Paul to the Galatians and Ephesians*, tr. William Pringle (Grand Rapids: Baker Book House, 1993), 215–16.
7. Paul Tillich, *Systematic Theology: Three Volumes in One* (Chicago: University of Chicago Press, 1967), vol. 2, 162.
8. Alexander Campbell, *The Christian System* (Cincinnati: H. S. Bosworth, 1866), 172–73.
9. Clark M. Williamson, "Preaching the Easter Faith," *Encounter* 37 (1976), 48.
10. Christopher Morse, *Not Every Spirit: A Dogmatics of Christian Disbelief* (Valley Forge, Pa.: Trinity Press International, 1994), 160.
11. "The Design for the Christian Church (Disciples of Christ), in *Chalice Hymnal* (St. Louis: Chalice Press, 1995), 355.
12. *Baptism, Eucharist, Ministry* (Geneva: World Council of Churches, 1982). This document has sparked an international ecumenical discussion chronicled in subsequent publications from the World Council of Churches.
13. Most of these associations are in Bernhard W. Anderson, "Water," *The Interpreter's Dictionary of the Bible*, ed. George R. Buttrick, et al. (Nashville: Abingdon Press, 1964), vol. 4, 806–10; cf. Mircea Eliade, *Patterns in Comparative Religion*, tr. Rosemary Sheed (New York: Sheed and Ward, 1958), 188–215.
14. Lars Hartman, "Baptism," *The Anchor Bible Dictionary*, ed. David Noel Freedman, et al. (Garden City, N.Y.: Doubleday, 1992), vol. 1, 583–94.
15. Martin Luther, "The Babylonian Captivity of the Church," in *Luther's Works*, ed. A. R. Wentz and Helmut T. Lehmann (Philadelphia: Muhlenberg Press, 1959), vol. 36, 58–59.
16. John Calvin, *Institutes of the Christian Religion*, ed. John T. McNeill, trans. Ford L. Battles (Philadelphia: Westminster Press, 1960), IV.14.1 (1277).
17. Alexander Campbell, *Christian Baptism: With Its Antecedents and Consequences* (Bethany, W. Va.: Published by Alexander Campbell, 1853), 256.
18. Alexander Campbell, "Tracts for the People, No. 18. Baptism, No. 10," *Millennial Harbinger* 4 (1847), 251.
19. Barton W. Stone, *Christian Messenger* 1 (January 1827), 59, cited in D. Newell Williams, *Barton Stone: A Spiritual Biography* (St. Louis: Chalice Press, 2000), 178.
20. "A Word to the Church on Baptism: Report of the Commission on Theology, 1987," in Clark M. Williamson, *Baptism: Embodiment of the Gospel*, The Nature of the Church Studies Series 4 (Indianapolis: Council on Christian Unity, 1987), 51–53; idem, *Way of Blessing, Way*

of Life: A Christian Theology (St. Louis: Chalice Press, 1999), 282–87; idem with Ronald J. Allen, *Adventures of the Spirit: A Guide to Worship from the Perspective of Process Theology* (Lanham, Md.: University Press of America, 1997), 199–201. For further discussion and liturgical materials for conducting baptism, see *Baptism and Belonging: A Resource for Christian Worship*, ed. Keith Watkins (St. Louis: Chalice Press, 1991).

21. Luther, "The Babylonian Captivity of the Church," 60.
22. Although these thoughts are discussed in various ways by other authors, they were inspired for me by Rebecca Button Prichard's theology of the senses in her *Sensing the Spirit: The Holy Spirit in Feminist Perspective* (St. Louis: Chalice Press, 2000).
23. For a representative guide to different ways of putting together sermons, see *Patterns of Preaching: A Sermon Sampler*, ed. Ronald J. Allen (St. Louis: Chalice Press, 1998).

Appendix: Relationships among Contemporary and Historic Theological Families

1. Fuller descriptions of these families can be found in my *Interpreting the Gospel: An Introduction to Preaching* (St. Louis: Chalice Press, 1998), 73–80.
2. Stanley Hauerwas and William Willimon, *Resident Aliens* (Nashville: Abingdon Press, 1989), 24.
3. For fuller descriptions, see Allen, *Interpreting the Gospel*, 24–28.
4. Those who need immediate start-up knowledge about preaching in their traditions can make good beginnings in *Concise Encyclopedia of Preaching*, edited by William H. Willimon and Richard Lischer (Louisville, Ky.: Westminster John Knox Press, 1995).
5. Robert P. Waznack, "Homily," *The New Dictionary of Sacramental Worship*, ed. Peter E. Fink, S.J. (Collegeville, Penn.: The Liturgical Press, 1990), 552–58.
6. John Wesley, *John Wesley's Works*, ed. Albert C. Outler (Nashville: Abingdon Press, 1984), vol. 1, 104.

Index

159

About the Author

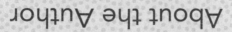

CAROLYN LARSEN has written more than forty books for children and adults. She is best known as the author of the Little Girls Bible Storybook line of products, which have collectively sold more than one million units. In addition, Carolyn is a speaker who has taught and spoken extensively in the United States and overseas. She is the cofounder of the performing group Flashpoints, which is composed of five women who share a God-ignited passion to encourage women and girls to know God better through drama, creative movement, signing, and humor. Carolyn is the mother of three and lives with her husband in Wheaton, Illinois.